DEVELOPING A
VISION
FOR MINISTRY

3RD EDITION

DEVELOPING A
VISION
FOR MINISTRY

AUBREY MALPHURS

BakerBooks

a division of Baker Publishing Group

www.BakerBooks.com

© 1992, 1999, 2015 by Aubrey Malphurs

Published by Baker Books
a division of Baker Publishing Group
P.O. Box 6287, Grand Rapids, MI 49516-6287
www.bakerbooks.com

Printed in the United States of America

Library of Congress Cataloging-in-Publication Data

Malphurs, Aubrey.
    Developing a vision for ministry / Aubrey Malphurs. — Third edition.
      pages cm
    Includes bibliographical references and index.
    ISBN 978-0-8010-1873-2 (pbk.)
    1. Mission of the church. I. Title.
    BV601.8.M32 2015
    253—dc23   2015014006

To
my wife and family
Susan
Mike
Jen
David
Greg

Contents

FOREWORD

In Robert Browning's poem "Paracelsus" a man travels toward a city, but it is surrounded by swirling mists. He thinks that he must have taken the wrong road and lost his way. But then the mist opens and for an instant he glimpses the spires of the city in the distance. Browning pens the triumphant lines:

> So long the city I desired to reach lay hid
> When suddenly its spires afar flashed through the circling
>   clouds,
> You may conceive my transport,
> Soon the vapours closed again, but I had seen the city!

A leader must have vision. We all see the shrouding mists, but leaders have seen the city. Leaders glimpse what others may not see and are captured by it. That's why they risk everything to reach the city.

Christian leaders do not have dreams in the night. Their visions belong to the day. Those who dream by night in the murky recesses of their minds wake and find their visions vanity; but the dreamers of the day are formidable men and women, for they receive their dreams from God with open eyes and they believe that under God they can turn them into reality.

Since our vision must be God's vision, we must gain it from the Scriptures. Some devout women and men, however, have taken an unauthentic lead from their commitment to the Bible. They long for "the good old days" of the church when God was alive and well and when he rolled up his sleeves and worked miracles. Their vision amounts to going back to "the New Testament church."

But which New Testament congregations do they have in mind? These early churches were infested with heretics. Members were at each other's throats. Some were guilty of sexual sin and many rejected apostolic authority. If our vision lies in a return to a New Testament church, then there's good news. We've already arrived!

Let's face it. There were no "good old days" for the church. There were no favorable times and no better saints than there are today. While we may learn from the past, we cannot copy it. A vision for the church in the twenty-first century cannot come from going backward into the future.

Our vision must arise from recognizing what the transcendent, contemporary God wants to do for his church and through his church today. Having seen that, leaders can then envision what God will do in the place they serve—the congregation at Fifth and Main in a particular community. Strong leaders possess a vision as great as God and as specific as a zip code.

Leaders also communicate their vision to those who serve Christ with them. John Ruskin spoke of that service when he observed, "The greatest thing a human ever does in the world is to see something and tell others what he saw in a plain way. Hundreds can talk for one who can think, but thousands can think for one who can see. To see clearly and tell others clearly is poetry, prophecy, and religion all in one."

Leaders lift people's eyes to what matters. By bringing the eternal into time, they summon Christians to a different kind of service, giving them a different perspective. Leaders must not only see the city but must also talk about it in plain words their followers can grasp and that grasp their followers.

Yet, seeing and communicating vision is not magic. Leaders can be better at leading than they are. Aubrey Malphurs has written this helpful, down-to-ministry book that guides a thoughtful reader in developing a vision and inspiring others with it. One sure test of whether or not you are a leader is this: Does a book like this inflame you with indignation or fire your imagination? Leaders with enough imagination to capture reality will wear out this book as they develop a vision for ministry in the twenty-first century.

As Christian leaders we have something in common with Walt Disney. Soon after the completion of Disney World someone said, "Isn't it too bad that Walt Disney didn't live to see this!" Mike Vance, creative director of Disney Studios, replied, "He did *see* it—that's why it's here."

Haddon W. Robinson
The Harold John Ockenga
Distinguished Professor of Preaching
Gordon-Conwell Theological Seminary

Introduction

Numerous leaders, whether in the church or the parachurch, struggle in their role as leaders. This is clearly reflected in the fact that Christian institutions across the land have arrived at the twenty-first century exhausted and gasping for breath. Ministering to and leading in today's world of the church and the parachurch is a leadership-intensive enterprise. Currently nine out of ten American churches are either plateaued or dying with no revival in sight. A considerable number of parachurch organizations are experiencing much the same. Not just anyone can assume leadership under these difficult circumstances.

Some set the number of churched on any given weekend early in the twenty-first century at around 17 percent of the population. To make matters worse, a number of cults and New Age religions, such as Wicca, are both filling the void and attracting some unchurched. Most important, we seem to be losing our youth. Some estimate that as many as 70 percent of young Protestant adults between the ages of eighteen and twenty-two have stopped attending church regularly. Why are they so important? Not only are they the future of the nation, but they are the future of the church. If the typical church in America were to go to a hospital emergency room, the doctors would be quick to put it on life support.

At the same time, there is hope. A new wind is blowing across the horizon of American Christianity. It is the wind of vision. God is presently infusing a number of new leaders in various Christian organizations across the land with a profound, significant vision for the future. *Vision* is a word that has been borrowed from the marketplace, but it is also a good biblical concept. It is timely and critical to leaders because vision has the potential to breathe fresh life into them and, thus, into their church or parachurch ministries. In short, there is hope, great hope, for leaders in the twenty-first century.

Vision is one of several critical concepts that have a great impact on a church's or parachurch's ministry. The others are core values, mission, and strategy. Figure 1 not only presents them but also shows how they relate to one another. A ministry's core values dictate why it does what it does. Thus its values will determine the vision.[1] The mission is what the ministry is supposed to be doing. Often the ministry's vision will be an expansion of its mission.[2] Finally, the strategy involves how a ministry will implement its mission and vision. Without a clear, practical strategy, a ministry will never realize its mission and vision.[3]

Vision in terms of ministry exists on both a personal and an institutional level. Personal vision concerns itself directly with the individual leader's unique design, which helps immensely in determining his or her future ministry direction. It comes as the result of discovering one's divine design from God. This unique design consists of spiritual gifts, natural talents, passion, temperament, leadership style, and so on. The discovery of personal vision helps Christians in general and leaders in particular determine their future place of ministry within the body of Christ.

Institutional or organizational vision relates directly to the ministry of a particular Christian organization, whether a church or a parachurch. Once leaders have determined their personal vision, they identify with a ministry organization that has an institutional vision most closely aligned with their personal vision. This has several advantages. One is that it lessens the likelihood of ministry burnout. Another is that through aligning with the similar vision of an institution, the leader's personal vision has a greater impact, because it has the institution behind it.

Both personal and institutional visions are essential. This book is designed to help leaders develop a unique institutional vision for the organization they lead or are a part of. To accomplish this goal it is necessary to take six steps that make up the envisioning process.

The first step is to realize the importance of having a ministry vision. Here the question to be answered is, How vital is vision to ministry? Chapter 1 presents specific reasons why vision is essential to the success of any ministry that desires to be on the cutting edge of what God is doing in the twenty-first century.

The second step is to understand the definition of a ministry vision. Exactly what are we talking about? What does the term *vision* mean when used of a ministry? Chapter 2 defines vision and explains its key ingredients.

The third step is the process of developing, or giving birth to, a vision. Chapter 3 focuses attention on the participants in the development stage. It answers the question, Who in the ministry is responsible for birthing the vision? Chapter 4 takes leaders through the process of creating a vision statement tailor-made for their ministry. It also explains how leaders can know when they have such a vision.

The fourth step is communicating the vision. It is not enough to have a good vision. Leaders must become and recruit others to be vision casters who cast and recast the vision in such a way that people are inspired to own and follow the vision. Chapter 5 presents various ideas to help leaders communicate their vision, including the use of social media.

In the fifth step visionary leaders implement their visions. This focuses on the important area of leadership and the careful, patient construction of a leadership team to implement the vision. Chapter 6 helps the leader recruit a committed, cooperative visionary team who will own the same vision and work together toward the realization of that vision. Chapter 7 also concerns the implementation of the vision through team building. However, this chapter focuses on empowering a committed, visionary team to overcome the obstinate obstacles they are sure to face on the way to the implementation of the vision.

The last step is the preservation of a vision. Visionary people must know how to recognize and handle opposition and its fruit, discouragement. Failure in this area results in early funerals, that is, the death of the vision and ultimately the ministry. The last chapter helps leaders recognize and deal with various threats to the implementation process.

Finally, I have included questions or worksheets at the end of the chapters to help you and your leadership team think about, discuss, and work through the contents of the chapter. I recommend that leaders first read through the book themselves. Then they would benefit by reading this book along with their ministry teams and discussing and applying its contents to their particular ministry situation.

1

It's a Must!

The Importance of a Vision

What has gone wrong with the typical pastor's ministry? Why have so many churches plateaued? What are the board members looking for when they want to know where the church will be five or ten years from now and what that will look like? Why are so many pastors preaching more but enjoying it less?

In general the problem is that the church and those with boards are looking for a leader. They want someone whom they can respect to lead them in the twenty-first century. In particular the problem is vision. The missing vital element in leadership is vision. To lead men and women, especially the hard chargers, pastors will need to articulate God's exciting, profound vision for the church's future.

Vision is crucial to any ministry. Ministry without vision is like a surgeon without a scalpel, a cowboy who has lost his horse, a carpenter who has broken his hammer. To attempt a ministry without a clear, well-articulated vision is to invite a stillbirth. Church and parachurch ministries may grow at the very beginning, but without

God's vision they are destined to plateau and eventually die. There are at least eleven reasons for this.

A Vision Clarifies Direction

A characteristic of far too many North American ministries in general and churches in particular is a lack of direction. They simply don't know where they are going, and many have not even thought about it. In *Leadership*, George Barna wrote of pastors and vision, saying that "only 2% could articulate the vision for their church." He concludes, "That's one reason so many pastors are ineffective; they don't know where they're going."[1] If they do not *know* where they are going—a lack of mission—then surely they cannot *see* where they are going—a lack of vision. The problem with not knowing or seeing where you are going is that you are liable to wind up just anywhere, and "just anywhere" will not do in today's world that is so desperately in need of God's direction.

A critical question that every church and parachurch ministry must ask and revisit at least once a year is the *directional* question, Where are we going? Or better, Where does God want us to go? Where is he leading us? The answer is both the ministry's mission and vision. The mission determines what the direction is, while the vision, in particular, concerns what that direction looks like. It is important that leaders such as pastors and their people both know and see the future of their ministries. Why?

Leaders must be able to articulate what God has called them to do. Not being able to do so is to invite disaster. Some people will follow a so-called leader who does not know where he is going, but the result is that they all wind up in the proverbial ditch. Also, a leader cannot develop a plan to implement the ministry without a clear target. As someone has said, "If you aim at nothing, you will hit it every time."

On numerous occasions leaders in the Bible demonstrated a leadership based on clear ministry direction. Moses demonstrated his acute knowledge of God's direction for the people of his generation when he appeared before Pharaoh and demanded their release (Exod. 5–11). Nehemiah demonstrated that he knew precisely where he was going when he presented his vision to King Artaxerxes (Neh. 2:5).

The people who are a part of the organization must also know where it is going. People cannot focus on fog. If God's people are to accomplish great things for him, they must know what it is they are setting out to accomplish.

Most people who are a part of a ministry organization fall into one of three problematic categories of ministry direction. The largest category by far consists of ministries that have no vision and thus no idea where the ministry is headed other than to love people. Most often they are maintenance ministries that are headed nowhere. Neither the leaders nor the members have any direction. If the organization is a parachurch ministry and dependent on outside funding, it will soon die. However, if it is a church, it may continue several years in this condition until the majority of the members die off and there is no one to replace them.

Another problematic category consists of ministries with multiple directions. These are organizations led by a leadership team in which each member has his or her own unique vision for the ministry. One may envision an evangelism orientation for the ministry. Another may envision a discipleship orientation. While there is nothing wrong with any of these visions, an organization can sustain only a single ministry vision. Usually a ministry with multiple visions ends with a split. Actually the split was already cooking on the back burner from the very beginning of the organization; it only needed sufficient time to boil over and cause a major ministry disaster.

A final problematic category is ministries with a single, clear vision. In this case, the problem is that the vision is the wrong vision. An example would be a parachurch ministry whose vision is the Great Commission (Matt. 28:19–20; Mark 16:15). While many parachurch ministries have sprung into existence because of some major inadequacy in the church, this does not mean that God intends to replace the church with the parachurch. By definition the parachurch is to minister alongside the church, not in place of the church. And it may focus on some aspect of the church's vision, such as evangelization, but will not embrace a Great Commission vision that includes evangelism and much more.

Another example would be a church whose vision is not the Great Commission but some element of the commission. For example, one church is known in a community for its in-depth Bible teaching, another for its outstanding pulpiteer. A third church has a reputation for a strong family ministry, while a fourth has an outstanding counseling program. These attract people to what I call "bunny hop" or "consumer" Christianity. Many times the result is transfer growth—populating the larger churches at the expense of depopulating the smaller churches in the area. Another result is that people shop around the various churches according to present felt needs without any commitment to a particular body.

By way of contrast, early in his ministry Nehemiah made a point of communicating a mission and a vision to the people under his leadership, the remnant in Jerusalem, so that they would know precisely where they were going (Neh. 2:17–18). Joshua did the same shortly after he replaced Moses as the leader of Israel (Josh. 1:10–11).

A Vision Invites Unity

Scripture places great emphasis on the importance of unity among God's people. Indeed, God has sprinkled passages on unity throughout the Bible (Ps. 133:1; Rom. 15:5; Eph. 4:3, 13; Col. 3:14). An institutional vision is one of the critical components of unity in ministry. The vision affects at least two areas of organizational unity.

The first area of unity is the recruitment of ministry personnel. A vision signals to all who desire to be a part of the ministry precisely where that ministry is going. It is a portrait of the ministry's future.

20

This gives potential participants an opportunity to both examine and determine their own personal visions in light of their gifts, passions, temperaments, talents, and abilities. They can decide in advance if their personal vision closely matches the organization's direction or whether they should look elsewhere for ministry opportunities. In either case, this recruitment protects continued ministry cohesion because it heads off potential problems before they are conceived and brought into the ministry.

The second area of unity is the retention of ministry personnel. When there is a common vision, there will be harmony on the ministry team. New Testament ministry is team ministry (see, for example, Acts 11:22–30; 13:2–3, 5; 15:40; 16:1–3).[2] A good ministry team consists of richly gifted people with diverse personalities who make significant but different contributions to the ministry. This is the reason wise leaders will recruit staff members who have strong gifts in areas where the leaders are less gifted. The problem is that this diversity supplies the fuel for potential conflict among those on the ministry team. Each temperament has a different perspective on life and, therefore, a different opinion about how things should be accomplished.

The solution to this problem is a clear, single ministry vision. Vision functions as a cohesive factor; it holds the team together. The team consists of people who are creatively different, but a major reason they joined the team initially is because they held passionately to the same vision. If the vision is nurtured carefully, the result is that each person appreciates and values the other because he or she sees how each, though different, is necessary and contributes in a unique way to the accomplishment of their vision. They realize that they all need each other if anything significant is going to take place. This, in effect, mirrors such passages on the importance of diversity within unity as 1 Corinthians 12:20–22 and Ephesians 4:15–16.

Vision is vital to another area of the retention of ministry personnel. If regularly communicated, the vision serves as a constant reminder to those in the ministry of the direction they have agreed to pursue together as a team. This is important because life is full of changes. Often people and ministries change and adjust their direction. Clarity of the vision gives the people who make up the organization a chance to reevaluate the organization's direction in light of their own gifts and personal direction in life. If the forecast is eventual disharmony, a person can seek another opportunity more in line with his or her own vision. But whether a person contemplates joining the organization or is already involved in that organization, a clear knowledge of ministry direction best enhances organizational harmony.

A Vision Facilitates Function

Another characteristic of many ministries today is that they do not know what they are supposed to be doing. They do not have a biblical mission. Others have strayed, having chosen maintenance over mission. For example, one denominational executive was overheard saying sarcastically, "The church is organized for the 1950s, and if the 1950s ever come again, we will be ready." This is especially true of the church in North America and Europe. If the typical business in the marketplace did not know what it was supposed to be doing (and some do not) or strayed, then it would not last long before going out of business. Some shrewd observers of American Christianity feel that for all intents and purposes the church has all but gone out of business.

A question that every ministry must regularly ask and revisit is the functional question, What are we supposed to be doing? Your vision, as well as the mission, answers this question. What the vision does uniquely for the ministry is to paint a portrait of what God intends for the ministry to accomplish so that all can see it.

The answer to the functional question for the church is the Great Commission. In Matthew 28:19 Jesus commands that the church "make disciples." This involves moving people from prebirth to maturity—from raw paganism to a compelling Christlikeness. Prebirth refers to that period of time before the new birth (John 3:3). The church is to pursue lost people, win them to Christ, and then move those new and the older disciples to spiritual maturity. But what does this look like? Vision communicates all this but does so pictorially. It provides people with a picture of what this process looks like. This is critical because if people cannot see it, then it probably will not happen.

A Vision Enhances Leadership

A question on the minds of many in ministry is, Where are the leaders? North American Christianity is facing a time in its history when many older Boomer leaders who have served well in the church at home and on the mission field are reaching retirement age. The question thus becomes who will replace them? The answer is today's Millennial generation and that of tomorrow. But what is essential to this new leadership? What will mark them and others as leaders?

One answer is vision. Developing a vision and then living it vigorously and authentically are essential elements of leadership. I define a leader as a godly servant (character) who knows and sees where he or she is going (mission and vision) and has followers (influence). That describes not only the Savior but also his disciples and those who ministered in the early church as recorded in Acts.

This definition reveals several characteristics. First, godly servants are people who display Christlike character throughout the ministry organization. They are people of integrity who exhibit the fruit of the Spirit (Gal. 5:22–23) and engender trust. They are in ministry not because of what it can do for them but to serve others on behalf of the Savior. Second, they know and see where they are leading their ministries. They have a dynamic mission that enables them to know where they are going and, most important, a clear, energizing vision that helps them see that direction. Third, the result of godly, Christ-like character and a powerful, compelling vision is influence. And it is influence that attracts and catalyzes followers (a good one-word definition of leadership is influence). When a congregation has a leader who owns a vision and powerfully lives that vision in a Christ-like manner, they will follow that leader to the ends of the earth.

A Vision Prompts Passion

One of the problems that leaders face in their ministries—especially in today's smaller, struggling churches—is the mediocrity problem. They are not giving enough attention to what they do and how they do it. For example, Sunday mornings tend to be poorly planned and poorly executed. I recall how in one church, the person leading worship rushed in just a few minutes before the service and asked, "What hymns should we sing this morning?" The church constantly faces this temptation in dealing with its people.

Over a period of years, the church can allow itself to lapse into a maintenance mentality—it just seems to be getting by. Over time this leads to ministry mediocrity. Every Sunday it is business as usual. The people come to church but may seem to be going through the motions. When they leave, not much has happened to them and not a lot takes place spiritually in their lives during the week. The younger generations will not tolerate this, and many are leaving their churches, searching for greener spiritual pastures. A major reason for all this is a general absence of passion for the church and its ministry.

Vision and passion work hand in hand. While *vision* is a seeing word that involves what leaders see in their heads, *passion* is a feeling word that involves their emotions—what they feel in their hearts. Passionate people are those who feel strongly about something. The "something" in this context is the vision. An exciting, compelling vision fuels passion. When leaders get a vision from God and they see what their churches could be and what he has in mind for the ministry, something marvelous happens—that vision usually results in a virile, infectious sense of passion. Not only do people know and see what they are supposed to be doing, but they can feel it as well. And if enough people catch the vision and experience this passion, it is possible that the ministry can re-create itself to become more effective in mission. An example of a vision-impassioned leader was Paul, who was so inflamed by his vision of preaching the gospel where Christ was unknown (Rom. 15:20) that he was willing to be cursed and cut off from Christ for the sake of Israel—that they might know Christ (9:3–4).

A Vision Fosters Risk Taking

A shared vision fosters risk taking by a congregation. People with a compelling, passionate vision are willing to take risks that they might not otherwise take. While this is especially true in ministries such as church or parachurch planting, it applies to other ministry situations as well.

When the point person or lead pastor casts the vision, everyone knows what needs to be done—they can see it in their heads. That is not the question. The question is, How will we accomplish it? Sometimes you know the answer, but more often you do not. Consequently, ministry for Christ becomes an exciting venture of faith into the mystery of God's unknown. You may attempt something for Christ that does not work. However, rather than throwing in the proverbial towel in despair and walking away, you attempt something else and it does work. Though much of what you are doing is experimental, it is not ambiguous. The vision makes it clear to all the reason you are doing it. It is for God and the Savior.

People are not asking for guarantees. Most are aware that no guarantees exist, yet they are committed to Christ and the ministry anyway. The risks are great, but so is the God they serve as well as the vision he has given them (Rom. 11:33–36). How else can we explain

25

the early church and what God accomplished through them, or those believers who make up the faith hall of fame in Hebrews 11? They all were willing to take vision-engendered risks.

A Vision Offers Sustenance

Ministry can be very difficult, even painful. Just ask those who minister on a full-time basis. Discouragement and disappointment can lurk in the ministry hallways and boardrooms of the typical church or parachurch ministry. It is not beyond the enemy to incite persecution against Christ's church (Acts 8:1). Spiritual warfare comes with the ministry territory (Eph. 6:10–18). Many have risked or given their lives for the Savior and the furtherance of the gospel (read Hebrews 11).

The list of martyrs for the cause of Christ is extensive. But what has sustained Christians, from the beginning of the church in the book of Acts to the church today? What has kept people like Paul, Peter, James, Calvin, Luther, the Wesleys, Billy Graham, and many others on track? One answer is a clear, biblical vision. It encourages people to look beyond the mundane and the pain of ministry. It holds a picture in front of them that distracts them from what is and announces loudly, "This is what could be." All the trouble and grief that we experience in this world while serving the Savior are trivial compared to the importance of what we are attempting through him and for him. That picture carried in our mental file is one of God's means for sustaining us in the worst of times.

A Vision Creates Energy

Not much happens without an inspiring, compelling vision. Not much was happening in Nehemiah's day. The people had no vision. Jerusalem lay in ruins, and no one was motivated to do anything about it (Neh. 1:3). Then along came Nehemiah with a mission and a vision from God to rebuild the gates and walls of the city.

Visions are exciting and energizing—they energize people. They strike a spark—the excitement that lifts a ministry organization out of the mundane. They supply the fuel that lights the fire under a congregation; they enable leaders to stop putting out fires and start igniting fires. A vision from God has the potential to turn a maintenance mentality into a ministry mentality. And when your vision resonates with your values and mission, it generates the energy that fuels the accomplishment of the ministry task.

How does a vision generate such energy? One way is that it inspires people. The vision of people coming to Christ or developing spiritual maturity touches them and moves them to action. They realize that the total transformation of one's life toward Christlikeness is what ministry is all about (Col. 1:28–29). Also, the dream challenges them. Many have languished in ministry because no one has challenged them to charge the enemy's fortresses. Many are caught up in what is, and no one has cast a vision of what could be. A leader with a compelling sense of vision from God challenges people to get up and move out of personal mediocrity and accomplish something meaningful for the risen Savior.

A Vision Provides Purpose

The right vision creates meaning in people's lives. It gives them a sense of divine purpose in life—of being a part of something great, something bigger than themselves that God is accomplishing at this time and place in history. And it is something that will bring glory to him.

With a shared vision, people see themselves not just as congregants or pew warmers, taking up space, but as a vital part of a church that is exerting a powerful impact on a lost and dying world. They are not simply in a church taking a walk; they are on a crusade. They are part of a revolution that has the potential to change this world—to have a wonderful impact for Christ.

What does this look like? If you were to ask a person what he or she does in church, some would answer, "I am a teacher of adolescents." However, others involved in the same ministry would answer, "I am changing the life course of a class of adolescents who will someday accomplish great things for Christ." What is the difference? The latter have a vision that brings a sense of purpose that, in turn, gives meaning to their lives. They see the big picture and how they fit into it. The result is commitment and dedication to God and a sense of personal significance that is found only in Christ.

A Vision Encourages Giving

An often ignored truth in ministry circles is that a vision is the key to people's giving of money. Many organizations attempt to raise funds by appealing to their constituency on the basis of need and not vision. The problem is that most people are not motivated to give to meet needs. If need motivated giving, then most people would be givers and most ministries would not have any financial shortages.

Wise donors view giving as a serious investment of God's money. Many donors view giving to ministries that constantly appeal primarily on the basis of need much the same as investing in an organization that is in the red. People do not want to give regularly to bail out a ministry that faces or has been inundated with debt. They question the reason for the debt. Does this mean the ministry is no longer making a difference for Christ? Is there any future for this ministry?

People are moved to give to organizations that project an exciting, well-articulated vision of what they believe is God's future for them. The vision says the ministry is not static but dynamic. It is going somewhere. It is not hopelessly trapped in the cobwebs of yesterday's debts but is focused on the exciting possibilities of the future. Vision communicates that while God is doing something exciting now, the best is yet to come.

Not only does vision motivate people to give of their finances or treasure, but it also encourages them to give of their time and talent. Both are critical to the life of any ministry organization. Most ministry organizations depend heavily on volunteers. Yet today's generation is so short on extra time for ministry that they are not able to use their talents for ministry effectively. They cherish their time and, therefore, many will give of their treasure before their time and talents when actually all three are needed.

After Nehemiah communicated his vision, the people of God responded not only with their treasure (Neh. 7:70–72) but also with their time and talents (detailed in Nehemiah 3). Most likely this happened because vision ultimately affects people's values and felt needs. People find time in their busy schedules for that which matters. Nehemiah's people valued the concept of rebuilding the city gates because their dilapidation symbolized the spiritual decline of Israel at that time. People also respond to visions that address their felt needs. Nehemiah's vision found his people in dire need of deliverance from their distress and reproach (1:3).

> **ELEVEN REASONS VISION IS IMPORTANT**
> 1. Clarifies direction.
> 2. Invites unity.
> 3. Facilitates function.
> 4. Enhances leadership.
> 5. Prompts passion.
> 6. Fosters risk taking.
> 7. Offers sustenance.
> 8. Creates energy.
> 9. Provides purpose.
> 10. Encourages giving.
> 11. Motivates the congregation.

A Vision Motivates the Congregation

Perhaps one of the most important reasons if not the most important reason that vision is so important to a church is that a good vision motivates the congregation with a desire to pursue and realize the church's mission—to make disciples. My observation is that today more churches have a mission statement than churches did in the late twentieth century. Somehow along the way, they are picking up on the importance of knowing where they are going. So I am not surprised when consulting with a church to discover that it has a mission. It may not be a good one, and no one may be able to recall what it is; nevertheless, they and others like them can proudly produce what for them is a mission statement.

Simply having such a statement alone does not mean that a church will make disciples. They must address the question, Are we merely a church with a vision, or are we a truly visionary church? Something must excite and motivate people to want to realize the mission, and that something is the vision. This is so important to the church's future that I cover it more in depth in the next chapter, where I define a vision.

QUESTIONS FOR REFLECTION AND DISCUSSION

1. This chapter presented eleven reasons a vision is important to a church or parachurch ministry. Did it convince you of the necessity of having such a ministry vision? Why or why not?

2. Did any of the eleven reasons seem more important than the others—at least to you? If so, which ones? Why?

3. Would any of the eleven reasons for a vision help your ministry? If no, why not? If yes, how?

4. There are other reasons a vision is important. What are some that come to your mind or came to your mind as you read this chapter? What other reasons would you add to the list?

2

WHAT ARE WE TALKING ABOUT?

The Definition of a Vision

Chances are good that you have attended one of the many conferences on leadership. On numerous occasions I have noted that most of the conference speakers use terms such as *culture, strategy, systems, missional, disciple,* and *vision.* When I hear them I want to raise my hand, interrupt the speaker, and ask him or her to define their terms. (Actually I did this at one conference and was shocked when the speaker, whom you all would know, confessed that he could not define the term he was using.) You see, most speakers assume that we understand what they mean. My guess is that most of us do not. And if we do not understand, then the speakers are not communicating as they must. Speakers and their listeners are not connecting at all.

In the last chapter we saw how important vision is and that it plays a critical role in the leadership and very survival of our ministries. Now I want to define the term *vision* so you will know what I am talking about when I use it. I refer to this as a "clarity moment" and attempt to do this when speaking and writing to clarify my use of terminology and avoid miscommunication. See if you agree with my definition of *vision*.

When defining a concept, I find it helpful to examine what it is not before examining what it is, and that is the route I will use in the following. First, we will examine what a vision is not and then what it is. Finally, this definition will provide us with a vision audit that will help us assess our vision statements.

What a Vision Is Not

Several terms have been used synonymously with but are not the same as *vision*. They are *dream*, *goal*, *objective*, *purpose*, and *mission*.

A Vision Is Not a Dream

Dr. Martin Luther King Jr. used the terms *dream* and *vision* interchangeably in his famous "I Have a Dream" speech. I often use the terms as synonyms in this book.

The terms may be used synonymously, but, in fact, a dream is much broader than a vision. The envisioning process may begin with a dream, and dreams initiate or fuel visions. Indeed, most great visions are products of people who dream great dreams.

When helping leaders develop a vision, I usually begin by asking them what they dream about. I ask, "What do you see in your mind when you think about your ministry in terms of the future? What do you see when you think and pray about what could be?" If they see very little, I encourage them to set aside some time in their schedules on a regular basis to pray and seek God's direction regarding the future of their ministries. During this time they should dream about the future and answer questions such as, If God would grant me one wish concerning my future ministry, what would it be? This practice enhances the dream process.

A Vision Is Not Goals and Objectives

Two other terms that may be equated with *vision* are *goals* and *objectives*. There are several differences here. Goals and objectives are cold and abstract and do not warm the heart. A vision, however, is warm and concrete and has the potential to melt the coldest heart. Just as a dream precedes a vision, so a vision precedes goals and objectives. Goals and objectives follow a vision and are integral parts of the strategic plan that ultimately brings about the realization of the vision.

A Vision Is Not a Purpose

It's not unusual for the term *purpose* to be confused with *vision*. At first glance the two appear indistinguishable, and this may be the case depending on their usage, but there can be a subtle difference in meaning. In most cases purpose answers the question why? Vision answers the question what? Whether or not there is a difference depends on how a ministry answers these two questions. The reason a ministry exists may be the same as or different from what the ministry seeks to accomplish for Christ. I argue that the purpose of the church is to glorify God (Rom. 15:6; 1 Cor. 6:20), whereas the mission and vision of the church concern the Great Commission (Matt. 28:19–20). Others wed purpose and vision.

A Vision Is Not a Mission

A fifth term that is confused with *vision* is *mission*, but the terms are different in many ways. A ministry's mission is a statement of where it is going, whereas its vision is a picture or snapshot of the same. Primarily the mission affects planning the organization's future, while the vision affects the communication of that future. A mission statement is short—no longer than a sentence. A vision can be short or long, ranging in length from one sentence to several pages. The purpose of the mission is to inform people as to where

33

the ministry is going. The purpose of the vision is to excite and motivate them to want to get there. The mission involves the activity of doing or accomplishing the organization's future, whereas the vision involves seeing in one's head that future. The source of the mission is the head—the mission stimulates the mind. The source of the vision is the heart—the vision is an emotional thing. It stimulates the emotions. A mission can be taught, but a vision is more caught than taught.[1]

What a Vision Is

I define a vision as a clear, exciting picture of the future of a ministry, such as a church, that God uses to motivate that ministry to accomplish its mission. It has four vital facets.

A Vision Is Clear

You must not expect people to act on information they do not understand. To paraphrase the apostle Paul, if the bugle boy muffs the call to arms, what soldier will know to prepare himself for battle? (1 Cor. 14:8). While a well-developed vision statement has the potential to accomplish a number of important spiritual objectives, it accomplishes nothing unless it is clear and easily understood. If the people who make up the ministry do not or cannot understand the vision, then there is no vision, regardless of the amount of time spent developing it. The immediate goal is to blow away any mental cobwebs and vacuum any mental dust that might clutter the comprehension of the dream.

This raises the obvious question: How can you know if the vision is clear? A vision is clear when those who are a part of the ministry understand it well enough to articulate it to someone else. Therefore it is wise periodically to quiz various individuals in general and the leadership in particular to determine their understanding of the vision.

Ask them such questions as, Where is this ministry going and what will it look like when it arrives? What would you like to see this ministry accomplish? What do you think this work will have accomplished five years from now? If people look puzzled or stammer and stutter, then your vision is obtuse and in need of clarity.

EIGHT DIFFERENCES BETWEEN A MISSION AND A VISION

	Mission	Vision
Definition	Statement	Snapshot
Application	Planning	Communication
Length	Short	Short or long
Purpose	Informs	Excites
Activity	Doing	Seeing
Source	Head	Heart
Experience	Intellectual	Emotional
Development	Science	Art
	(Taught)	(Caught)

Next, leaders must communicate the vision as clearly as possible so that their people understand what God's desire is for them. Moses is a case in point. He could not have missed God's mission for his people in Egypt. God spoke face-to-face with Moses when he declared his plan to liberate Israel from Egyptian bondage and lead them into "a good and spacious land, to a land flowing with milk and honey" (Exod. 3:8). What did Moses see and say to his people? What vision did he see in response to this God-ordained mission? The answer is found in such places as Exodus 13:5; Deuteronomy 8:7–9; 11:9. Deuteronomy 8:7–9 is noteworthy:

> For the LORD your God is bringing you into a good land—a land with brooks, streams, and deep springs gushing out into the valleys and hills; a land with wheat and barley, vines and fig trees, pomegranates, olive oil and honey; a land where bread will not be scarce and you will lack nothing; a land where the rocks are iron and you can dig copper out of the hills. (NIV)

This is what Moses saw. An important question is, What do you see? This description evokes all kinds of pictures that can fire the imagination. However, the most important question is, What did his followers, the Israelites, see?

The problem was with Moses's feelings of inadequacy to communicate the plan. Consequently, God instructed Moses to use Aaron as his "mouthpiece" until Moses was ready to assume the task (Exod. 4:16).

Regardless of Moses's feelings or our feelings, the goal of clarity is to discover the essence of the vision and present it in specific, concrete terms.

A Vision Is Exciting

I tell my church-planting students that if their people are not excited about the potential to birth a new church, then they need not go any farther. It is not going to happen. The same is the case for implementing a biblical vision. Vision is like caffeine for the soul—it has the potential to keep you awake at night. No excitement translates into no vision. The problem for too many ministry visions is that, once they are conceived and born, they don't excite anyone and thus face quick, untimely deaths and are quietly buried in some vision graveyard (the church's filing cabinet). If people are not excited by the vision, there really is no need to proceed any farther. It's time to go back to the vision drawing board and/or get help.

I have worked with several ministries in developing a vision for their organizations. Most quit too soon. They begin the process with little idea of the time and energy necessary to develop a good vision. The result is a premature product that moves no one. Leaders must ask, Am I stimulated by our vision? They must realize that if they are not excited by the final product, then other people in the organization will not be excited either.

People in general and pastors in particular need to understand that God uses vision-produced excitement to motivate people to pursue aggressively the church's mission—to make disciples. If you get anything from this book on vision, you must get this. It is the reason a church must have both a mission and a vision. The mission tells the congregation where they are headed, and the vision serves to excite them and motivate them to want to go there. If there is no vision, then the mission will likely not be accomplished. The mission by itself cannot sustain the excitement necessary to motivate its realization and implementation.

Some expect the church's mission (to make disciples) to do the work of the vision—to excite and thus motivate the people. They think that by merely coming up with a good, biblical mission statement, its implementation will take care of itself. This is possible but tends not to work that way. It takes the vision to fire up the mission. According to Matthew 28:19, the biblical mission for the church is to make disciples. And no matter how you say it, the mission will grow old and stale without a fresh, exciting vision that builds a fire beneath it.

If a congregation has a biblical mission but the people are not excited about it, then there is a vision problem. In fact, you can judge where people are based on their excitement over the vision. The continuum below serves as a vision barometer to help you determine where you are in terms of your vision and the excitement it generates in the people. The idea here is to move people from wherever they are on the continuum to where they need to be.

Vision Barometer

No excitement	Some excitement	Growing excitement	Most excited

When the people's excitement falls any place on the left side of the barometer, it indicates that there's not enough excitement to initiate and sustain the vision. When it's any place on the right, the excitement will sustain the vision. Keep in mind that just because your people land on the right side and are excited about the church's vision, this doesn't mean that your work is done. You are dealing with people's emotions, which can shift up or down. This means that to maintain the vision, pastors and their staffs and boards must be constant vision casters. I have heard Rick Warren say that it takes only a month to forget the vision. I think he is correct; therefore a primary job of the pastor and staff is to be casting the vision at every opportunity in every way possible. I will say more about vision casting in chapter 5.

A Vision Is a Mental Picture

Vision is a seeing word. A good vision probes the imagination in such a way that it develops visual representations in the mind. John R. W. Stott says of vision, "It is an act of seeing—an imaginative perception of things, combining insight and foresight. . . . We see what it is—but do we see what could be?"[2]

Visionaries have the innate ability to see what others do not see. While they see needs, they have the natural capacity to see beyond those needs to the unique, exciting opportunities those needs present. For example, a nonvisionary person drives through urban or suburban America and sees apartments, houses, and men, women, and children. A visionary person drives through the same area and sees future ministries, possible meeting sites, even a potential congregation.

Moses led the people of God in the wilderness with a picture in his mind of the Israelites living and serving God in the Promised Land "flowing with milk and honey." It is interesting to note that the end of Deuteronomy records that shortly before Moses's death, God took him up on Mount Nebo to show him the Promised Land (34:1–4). This land was a vital component of God's covenants and promise and the ultimate realization of the vision (Exod. 3:8). While God had several purposes in mind for doing this, I suspect he wanted Moses to see the physical reality of what he had seen in his mind and dreamed about all those years in the wilderness. It was God's physical, visible assurance to Moses that the dream was about to become a reality, even though Moses would not be a part of it.

The Eskimos in the cartoon below are visionaries—visionary pioneers. As we look at the cartoon, the question is not what do *we* see? The question we must ask is what do *they* see? The obvious answer is an igloo even though they are standing in a sweltering, arid desert. They are carrying around a snapshot of an igloo in their mental files. That means that what is now a desert will include an igloo. A second more important question is what do you see—a desert or a desert with an igloo in it? Visionaries see an igloo in the desert where others see only the desert. So what is your igloo?

We'll build the igloo here!

A Vision Is the Future of the Ministry

Vision is always cast in terms of the future. Marcus Buckingham says, "What defines a leader is his preoccupation with the future. In his head he carries a vivid image of what the future could be, and this image drives him on."[3] It is a mental picture of what tomorrow will look like. It is a view of a ministry's future and its exciting possibilities.

Visionary leaders spend a large proportion of time thinking about and living in the future. In doing so they largely determine their future. By cultivating institutional visions, leaders have a vital part in inventing and influencing the future of their ministries. They know precisely the kind of ministry they want and where they are going with that ministry, and they press on toward the accomplishment of their goals.

However, this does not mean that visionaries ignore either the present or the past. Often they use the present as a platform to launch their ministries into the future. They may point to the status quo of the organization and use it to create dissatisfaction. Next, they envision a better future and rally people to join them in moving toward it.

But how do visionaries relate to the past? Wise visionaries learn from the past, but their very nature will not allow them to live in the past. For them living in the past would be comparable to driving a car by looking through the rearview mirror. An example is the apostle Paul, who states, "One thing I do: forgetting what lies behind and reaching forward to what lies ahead, I press on toward the goal" (Phil. 3:13–14).

Since the vision is the product of the visionary, it by nature is futuristic. Some visions are short-term visions, but as long as they exist, they concern the future. They are in a state of becoming right up to the point of their accomplishment; then they are over and done with. This was the case for Nehemiah. Rebuilding the walls was his vision until they were in place. At that point the vision was accomplished and ended abruptly. The same is true of Moses leading his people to the Promised Land and Noah building the ark. These short-term visions were very concrete and not open-ended.

Most visions, though, are perpetually in the state of becoming and thus remain futuristic. These are long-term or open-ended visions.

They are by nature broader, more abstract visions. An example is the Great Commission. The organizational mission of the church is the Great Commission, which includes pursuing, evangelizing, and discipling all people (Matt. 28:19–20). The church's vision is what that looks like as it accomplishes the mission. While a church that pursues this vision will win people, hopefully lots of people, it will never fully accomplish the vision. In a very real sense, this is a paradox, for the church is successfully accomplishing that which cannot be accomplished.

> **HOW A VISION RELATES TO THE FUTURE**
> - Short-term visions are eventually realized.
> - Long-term visions are in a constant state of becoming.

In general, most ministry organizations plan for a relatively lengthy existence. A vision is the key to any long-term existence. Therefore, ministries need to develop broad, long-term visions that are perpetually in the state of becoming.

Vision Essentials

Though not a part of my definition, there are at least two other characteristics of a vision that are important to a church or parachurch ministry. One is that a vision can be. The other is that a vision must be.

A Vision Can Be

A good vision drips with potential. It rests firmly on the bedrock of reality—thus it is highly feasible. The visionary leader possesses an uncanny sense of being on to something big for God, believing that God is planning something special and that the leader is a vital part of that plan.

Most often people and organizations err in one of two directions concerning the feasibility of a vision. On the one hand, there is little

41

or no vision. Most are moving in this direction. While consulting with churches, I encounter this problem repeatedly. One of the major reasons nine out of ten churches in America are either plateaued or dying is because they and their leadership have little or no vision. When it comes to vision, they drag their ministry heels. They do not see and thus do not know where they are going. For many this is due to a small-minded mentality. They do not think about and ask God for big things. But this is not a new problem. When Paul addresses the Christians in Ephesus, he slaps them lightly on the wrist for not thinking big enough when he says, "Now to Him who is able to do far more abundantly beyond all that we ask or think" (Eph. 3:20).

On the other hand, the vision may be too big. The problem here is twofold. Some people will not give the vision a fair hearing because it is so vast that it tends to overwhelm them. They feel intimidated and defeated just listening to the vision. Others who pursue a vision that is too big later become disillusioned and discouraged with the ministry. There develops a sense of futility that eventually leads to resignation from the ministry.

But how can you know when a vision is too big? This is difficult to determine because most visions are not big enough. Also, Jesus repeatedly rebukes the disciples for their lack of faith, not the fact that their faith is too big. Three issues affect the answer to this question.

The first issue is the visionary. Is he the right person to lead in accomplishing such a vision? People will question the visionary's character, credentials, and whether or not he is in the right position in the right organization to accomplish such a big vision. An example is Bill Bright, whose vision for Campus Crusade for Christ (now known simply as Cru) was to win the world to Christ in this generation. Most give his vision high marks because of who he is and what God has accomplished as far as the result of his vision.

The second issue is the visionary's people. It takes a big team to accomplish a big vision. Who is on the team? People will question their character and capability to realize the vision. An example of a team with high credibility is the men and women of Cru who are so committed and highly motivated that they are willing to go anywhere to win the world for Christ.

The third issue is whether the times are right for this vision. Is there any evidence that the world in general or a group of people in particular is ready to come to Christ? One of the problems in American Christianity is that many leaders do not understand their times. For example, they have missed the shift in America from a somewhat churched to a nonchurched culture and the implications of this for their

> **THREE ISSUES THAT AFFECT THE SIZE OF A VISION**
> 1. Who is the visionary?
> 2. Who are the visionary's people?
> 3. Are the times right for the vision?

ministries. Consequently, their visions take on an appearance of unreality because they show they are unaware of the needs and values of today's vast nonchurched generation.

A Vision Must Be

A good vision grabs hold and won't let go. Not only does the visionary believe that the vision can be, but he also is convinced that it must be. A critical sense of urgency dominates his thoughts. It might even keep him awake at night. He is so gripped by the vision that his spirit refuses to rest until the ministry is moving in the direction of the vision. Once you see and grasp what can be, you will never again be satisfied with what is. Several essentials contribute to this conviction.

One variable is the belief God is in it. He is the motivating force behind what the visionary wants to achieve. There is little question that God has placed this vision on his heart. He has committed his life to accomplishing God's will, and now God has revealed it in the form of the ministry dream. Nehemiah demonstrates this awareness of divine involvement when he says, "I did not tell anyone what my God was putting into my mind to do for Jerusalem" (Neh. 2:12).

A second variable is that God has chosen to accomplish this vision through this particular person. Perhaps God will use other leaders as well, but this person is convinced that God will use him to play a major role, just as God used King David to serve his divine purpose in David's generation (Acts 13:36).

But how does a visionary person know this is the case? One indication is that God grants him success as he moves to accomplish God's will. Some have described this as God opening the doors of opportunity. Nehemiah experienced this when pagan King Artaxerxes granted his request to leave and go to Jerusalem to pursue his vision. The granting of this permission was so unlikely that Nehemiah knew God had to be in it. Perhaps this amazement is reflected in the fact that later he makes two references to it. In Nehemiah 2:8 he says, "And the king granted them to me because the good hand of my God was on me." Then in verse 18 he says, "I told them how the hand of my God had been favorable to me and also about the king's words which he had spoken to me."

A third variable is that the vision will benefit people. A leader cares about people and is moved to believe that they will be better off because of the vision. In general, people will experience such benefits as eternal life, spiritual renewal, the healing of a marriage, reconciliation with a friend, and much more. And this only serves to excite and encourage the visionary even further. Dr. Martin Luther King Jr. believed that his vision had to be because it meant the liberation of black people in America from racism and oppression. Nehemiah reveals his heart for his people when he says in Nehemiah 2:17, "You see the bad situation we are in, that Jerusalem is desolate and its gates burned by fire. Come, let us rebuild the wall of Jerusalem so that we will no longer be a reproach."

Finally, the visionary is also convinced that the vision must be because of his passion for that vision. I mentioned this briefly in chapter 1. While *vision* is a seeing word, *passion* is a feeling word. It involves the emotions; it is what you feel strongly about. Vision and passion work hand in hand. Actually a good vision generates and fuels passion. As leaders and people begin to see what God wants them to accomplish and what their churches could be, this same vision elicits within them strong feelings toward that end. They become emotional about the vision. It moves them to the point where the vision is no longer a possibility but a must. And they discover that they will never be satisfied until they are on the way to seeing the realization of their vision. I suspect that it is this sense of passion that leads to the successful planting of some ministries and the revitalization of others. Without it, something vital is obviously missing, and people seem to be only going through the motions.

Also, as vision fuels passion, so passion, in turn, fuels charisma in many leaders. In chapter 5 I say more about charisma. For now, charisma concerns the leader's expressiveness. Passionate, visionary leaders with charisma have strong personal convictions that are reflected by authentic traits of self-confidence (Christ-confidence), expertise, strong dedication to the cause of Christ, and a genuine concern about people both saved and lost. They express or communicate all this through their behavior, personal appearance, demeanor, conversation, and in other ways. The result is that their leadership strongly attracts the attention of people and influences them for the ministry and the cause of Christ.

Summary

The Definition of a Vision

A vision is a clear, exciting picture of the future of a ministry, such as a church, that God uses to motivate that ministry to accomplish its mission.

The Vision Audit

We can use the definition of a vision to audit our vision and determine if it meets the criteria of a good vision statement. As you develop your vision and then later revisit that vision, ask the following questions:

1. Is the vision clear? Do the people in our ministry understand it?
2. Is it exciting? Does it motivate people to pursue our mission?
3. Does it create a picture in people's minds? Can they see it in their heads?
4. Is it future oriented? Does it present a picture of our ministry's future?
5. Do I believe that it can be? Is it feasible?
6. Am I convinced it must be? Am I passionate about it?

What have we learned so far? First, leaders should realize the importance of having a vision for their ministry organizations. Without a dream, the ministry is in trouble. Second, they should arrive at a clear definition of institutional vision so that they know precisely what it is they are about and to avoid any misunderstanding or miscommunication. Third, the vision must excite the people and motivate them to want to accomplish the ministry's mission. In the next chapter we begin the creative process of developing a unique vision for a ministry.

QUESTIONS FOR REFLECTION AND DISCUSSION

1. Does your ministry have a vision statement? If the answer is no, why not? How has this affected the ministry?
2. How would a clear, exciting vision help the ministry?

3. If your church or parachurch ministry has a vision statement, what is it? Does it excite your people?

4. Is it a short-term or long-term vision?

5. If you were to audit your vision, would it meet the criteria for a good vision statement? Is it clear? Is it exciting? Does it create a mental picture? Is it future oriented? Is it feasible? Are you convinced that it must be? If not, what is missing?

3

THE VISION PERSONNEL

Giving Birth to Your Vision, Part 1

Now that we realize the importance of a vision to one's ministry and have a definition for vision, the next question is, How does one go about developing the vision? And just as important, Who births the vision? Who is ultimately responsible?

Birthing a vision has much in common with birthing a child. Both events rely heavily on certain personnel and on the correct process. Before birthing a vision, one must ask two important questions: Who develops the vision or who are the personnel involved in the envisioning process? and How is the vision developed or what is the envisioning process?

This chapter answers the personnel question; the next chapter deals with the process question. Who takes responsibility for developing the vision? Initially the answer is the point person in the ministry. While that person does not develop the vision alone, he is responsible for guiding the process and making sure that there is a final product.[1] But who are these leaders, what is their role, and who else should be involved? In its focus on the vision personnel, this chapter answers all three questions.

The Point Person

The ministry leader is the sole point person or primary leader of the ministry. In the church this person is the senior or lead pastor. In the parachurch this individual goes by various titles, such as president or general director.

A Single Primary Leader

It is important to recognize that every ministry and every leadership team within a ministry needs a single primary leader. Today's emphasis on co-leadership, especially in the church where it is known as lay-elder rule, may be an attempt to be biblical but most likely is an overreaction to leadership by a single tyrant or despot, or in some cases to weak or unskilled professional leadership. Not only is the biblical foundation for co-leadership suspect—there is a problem with finding its biblical foundation—but the greater problem is that people cannot follow a group.[2] It is imperative that there be a single leader or a leader of leaders on a ministry team.[3]

The general leadership principle here is that where two or more relate together as a team (whether as a family, ministry, or some other relationship) for any period of time, one must stand out as the leader or head. Paul demonstrates this truth from a theological perspective in 1 Corinthians 11:3 where in a discussion of headship he says, "God is the head of Christ." The same idea is found in 1 Corinthians 3:23 and 15:28. The instructive principle to observe here is that even on the most perfect team in existence, the Trinity, there is headship. God the Father is the primary leader, the point person in the relationship.

From a practical perspective, all the participants in a ministry or on a leadership team are not equal in their leadership abilities, knowledge, experience, reputation, training, and commitment. Some are born with natural gifts of leadership and, in addition, may receive the spiritual gift of leadership (Rom. 12:6, 8). Others have been blessed and gifted in other areas for ministry. It is important that those with special leadership gifts and abilities take positions of primary leadership in the various organizations.

An Exciting Visionary Leader

A church or parachurch ministry's vision begins with and is the primary responsibility of the point person. And this individual benefits greatly if he or she is a visionary person. It takes a visionary leader to cultivate a profound, exciting vision of the future. What are the characteristics of visionary people? How would you know one if you saw one?

INTUITIVE

One characteristic that has surfaced among visionary leaders is a preference for relating to the world through intuition. Isabel Myers, one of the developers of the popular and widely used *Myers-Briggs Type Indicator* (MBTI), writes:

> Mankind is equipped with two distinct and sharply contrasting ways of perceiving. One means of perception is the familiar process of *sensing*, by which we become aware of things directly through our five senses. The other is the process of *intuition*, which is indirect perception by way of the unconscious, incorporating ideas and associations that the unconscious tacks on to perceptions coming from outside. These unconscious contributions range from the merest masculine "hunch" or "woman's intuition" to the crowning examples of creative art or scientific discovery.[4]

When Myers refers to sensing and intuition, she is discussing how people perceive or acquire information, how we master finding out about things. She believes that people have the ability to use both processes, and do use both, but prefer to use one more than the other. This she refers to as one's preference. People who prefer sensing acquire information through their eyes, ears, and other senses. They desire to discover what is actually there and is actually happening. These are the practical realists, the commonsense type of people in our world who focus on present reality.

However, people who prefer intuition gather information by looking beyond the senses to what some call a sixth sense. This sixth sense concerns the world of ideas, relationships, and possibilities, which for the intuitive-type person appear to flash out of nowhere. These people are future oriented and think not so much in terms of what is but what could be. They focus not on details and present realities but on the big picture and the exciting possibilities that lie in the future. In reviewing these characteristics, it becomes obvious that visionaries tend to favor the intuitive over the sensing process.

It is important to note at this point that neither process is good or bad. Both are necessary to the ultimate success and survival of any ministry. Every ministry needs both types, and it is the role of the intuitive types to take the lead in developing the organization's vision with input from the sensing types. Isabel Myers estimated that about 75 percent of the population in America prefers the sensing process and 25 percent the intuitive process, but samples collected by the professionals who administer and interpret the MBTI show that there are more intuitive-type people in the population than reflected in Myers's estimate.[5]

People can discover whether they prefer the intuitive or the sensing process in several ways. One subjective but fairly reliable approach is to read the above descriptions of the two processes and determine which fits. This assumes, of course, that a person has a good knowledge of how God has designed him or her. A more objective approach is to give these same descriptions to those who know the person well, such as a spouse or colleague, and ask their opinion. A third way is to take the MBTI, which is an instrument designed to help a person determine the preferred sensing or intuitive process and the strength of each as well as other preferences.[6]

Should you have difficulty finding someone who can administer the MBTI, another tool that is easier to obtain and less expensive is the *Kiersey Temperament Sorter*, which is a shorter version of the MBTI.[7]

Naturally the question arises, Can a person who prefers the sensing process change to prefer the intuitive process and become more visionary? Isabel Myers and professionals who have worked with the MBTI believe that children are born into this world with a predisposition for one process or the other. This results in a preference for that process, which means that individuals will develop and trust the one more often than the other as they take in information from the world.[8] We can infer that persons who by design prefer the sensing process can develop their intuitive abilities, but only to a limited degree. By their very nature they are best at using the sensing process. On the other hand, those who prefer the intuitive process can consciously develop and increase their ability to use this function and their visionary capacities to an even greater degree.

Does this mean that a sensing-type person cannot have a vision? The answer is no. Sensing-type people can catch a vision, but they go about it a different way. Whereas intuitive people naturally see a vision in their heads, sensing types have to see it literally with their eyes. They perceive it through their five senses—they see, smell, touch the vision. The way to help them catch a vision is to show them what you are talking about. If your vision is similar to that of another church or parachurch ministry, then take them to visit and see that ministry. This is the way they catch and then are able to communicate a vision.

This raises a question: Who should be the primary leader in an organization, the sensing- or intuitive-type person? The natural tendency among people in the ministry organization, or the vision community, is to follow the more visionary or intuitive-type leaders, because usually they have the unique and powerful ability to enable followers in ministry by communicating a unique, positive vision of the future. They display the strongest ownership of the vision and best personify the vision and tend to be most dedicated to it personally. Therefore, all things being equal, the intuitive-type leader would seem to have an edge over the sensing type when it comes to functioning as the point person or leader of leaders, but not always.

So we must ask, What should sensing-type leaders do? Is it okay for them to assume positions of senior leadership? And what about those who are already leading in the point position? The truth is that in the world of leadership all things are not equal. Sensing-type people may have leadership gifts and abilities from God as well as experience that intuitive types do not. As we wrote in our book *Re:Vision*, Gordon Penfold and I discovered through our research that a large number of sensing-type pastors are very good at revitalizing struggling churches. So if you are a sensing-type leader, do not prepare a letter of resignation or commence to clean out your desk. Instead, I would suggest that you consider the following. First, work hard at developing as much as possible your intuitive abilities. Second, visit and catch (as described above) the vision of a church that is similar to your own. Expose your senses to it in every way possible—remember, that is how you catch a vision. Then do your best to own and challenge your people with that vision. You may have to work harder at this than an intuitive-type leader, but with a little perspiration you can do it.

It may also be helpful to surround yourself with intuitive, visionary people and rely heavily on their skills and abilities. Remember, though, they cannot take your place as the keeper and caster of the vision, as most congregations will look to their leader and not other ministry personnel for this responsibility. You may decide to step down from the point position and defer to someone else better equipped or designed for this particular, unique role. This is the last and the most difficult option. It is for leaders who feel they can serve God and their congregation better in a support role rather than a lead role. God has wired them to be a support person, and being in the role of the point leader is very frustrating for them. The option of stepping down benefits them as individuals because it frees them to pursue areas within or outside the ministry for which they are better designed. The result of such a decision will be a greater sense of accomplishment and fulfillment with minimal burnout.

INFORMATION COLLECTOR

In addition to intuition, another characteristic of visionary-type people is their ability to recognize, collect, and synthesize pertinent information from a variety of sources. In short, they are great information collectors. One of my extremely gifted, visionary friends (who was in a high leadership position in a large ministry organization) has on several occasions with a big smile on his face referred to himself not as a pioneer but as a thief.

Jay Conger affirms this information-collecting role in *The Charismatic Leader* when he writes:

> I witnessed this same process among my own research subjects. The charismatic leaders were great information collectors with a difference—they used multiple and often apparently unrelated sources of information. Fred Smith says: "Mostly, I think, it is the ability to assimilate information from a lot of different disciplines all at once. Particularly information about change, because from change comes opportunity. . . . The common trait of people who supposedly have vision is that they spend a lot of time reading and gathering information, and then synthesize it until they come up with an idea."[9]

Essential to this information-collecting process is the information or knowledge gained from personal experience. In their book *The Leadership Challenge*, James Kouzes and Barry Posner indicate that intuition is the result of bringing together knowledge and experience.

This knowledge is not that which is gained in school but through hands-on experience in the marketplace. They conclude:

> Direct experience with the organization and the industry is the source of knowledge on how the organization and industry operate. Intuition, insight, and vision come from the knowledge that we acquire through direct experience and store in our subconscious.[10]

Thus visionary leaders should seek and value any knowledge gained from their experience in ministry. The emphasis, especially in academic circles in the American culture, is on knowledge gained from the classroom experience. From their research Kouzes and Posner conclude that knowledge gained from experience in the field contributes considerably more to the intuitive process. So, even when going to school, visionary leaders must pursue involvement in some form of ministry because of the contribution this experience makes to their understanding.

In light of the importance of ministry experience, some people point to the fact that a number of pastors of the larger churches in America are not seminary-trained people but individuals who came up through the ranks. I believe that, in general, this observation is correct. However, the key is to combine seminary training with good ministry experience in the field. Most reputable seminaries have field education programs that make provision for this during the leader's seminary years. In addition, a growing number of pastors early in the twenty-first century are focusing intentionally on developing leaders in their churches and including seminarians in the process. The real danger is to value the classroom experience over field ministry experience, which is a common occupational hazard for seminarians.

It is important that visionary leaders who desire to remain on the cutting edge of ministry expose themselves regularly to as many sources of information as possible. It is not merely a good idea for them to set aside time in their busy schedules for information collecting; it is a must. They are wise to read lots of books and articles on leadership, change, and so on. They can use podcasts and the social media as well. They should also attend selected conferences put on by the various visionary, hard-charging churches and organizations across the land that God is blessing. And it is very important that they value past ministry experience and seek more of the same in the future. Actually the ideal would be to pursue a yearlong, full-time internship in a ministry that God is obviously blessing. The experience gained from such an internship would be invaluable. All of these sources will supply the visionary leader with a constant flow of raw data for the intuitive mind to digest.

A discussion of the role of intuition in leadership may give the impression that whole ministry visions and entire new ministry directions pop full-blown into a visionary's mind at one sitting. In fact, this is rare. I believe that most visionaries combine the intuitive process in some fashion with the information-collecting process when envisioning the future of their ministries. Often the process of information collecting supplies the raw data on both the conscious and subconscious levels, which the intuitive mind takes and uses to perceive new relationships, new ways of doing things, and potent possibilities for the future.

What Does the Point Person Do?

Numerous unique ministry models exist that prescribe a leader's role in a particular Christian organization. While most attempt to be biblical, I suspect that other factors exert a strong influence on the leader's role or what he or she does in the point position. I am referring to such factors as the ministry community's expectations, the kind of ministry, the locale of the ministry, and so on. For example, a small church in the rural Midwest expects its pastor to have strong people skills, for much of his ministry will take place in homes, hospitals, and nursing homes. A larger church in an urban or suburban community in the East might expect its pastor to display strong skills in the areas of communication and administration.

In answering the question, What does the visionary leader do? I would like to add an element to his role as a primary leader. He must be the keeper of the vision. He takes responsibility for the vision. In this capacity, the leader wears at least three hats—cultivator, caster, and clarifier of the vision.

Vision Cultivator

The vision cultivator initiates and develops the organization's unique vision, which empowers the vision community for ministry. He begins the process by challenging the ministry to come up with a clear, exciting vision. At first he may develop the vision, but he also will solicit the input of others until it becomes everyone's vision.

Vision Caster

The vision caster functions as the primary vision communicator but is not the only vision communicator. Once the vision is cultivated and in place, the leader must take responsibility to keep it before the ministry community. He does this directly and indirectly through others in the ministry. Without the regular casting and recasting of the dream, people in the community are quick to stop dreaming and may behave as if there is no vision at all.

Vision Clarifier

Finally, as the vision clarifier, the leader focuses the vision. Cutting-edge organizations are characterized by a whirlwind of activity and cataclysmic change. In the midst of this, there must be someone who regularly rethinks and further refines the dream. He helps people comprehend the vision and discover their part in it. He supplies precision answers as to how, when, and where those in the vision community can play a significant role in the realization of the dream.

This clarification means periodic revisiting and rephrasing of the vision. In doing this the clarifier is not changing the vision but looking for new, creative ways to express it as a means of infusing fresh life and power into the dream. An example of this process in the marketplace is McDonald's hamburger chain. One way they have chosen to express their vision is by developing slogans. An example from the 1990s was "Food, Folks, and Fun." Their slogans are dynamic, not static, in that they are changed once or twice a year in an attempt to catch the public's eye afresh and sell more products.

In addition, clarification helps to determine if it is time to rethink and possibly change the dream. Fred Smith argues that the mark of a good leader is to "know when it's time to change the vision."[11] He gives as an indicator the demographic changes that can take place in the community and the church. Other indicators might be a change in leadership and/or the purpose of the organization.

Nehemiah is a good example of a sole, visionary leader who was able to cultivate, cast, and clarify a vision for the people of God in his day. It is interesting to note that in this situation God raised up a single leader, not a group of co-leaders who had no primary leader. People can follow only one visionary at a time. Nehemiah appears to have been an intuitive collector of vital information as evidenced by his nightly inspection trips described in Nehemiah 2.

> **THE FUNCTIONS OF A VISION KEEPER**
> - Vision cultivator
> - Vision caster
> - Vision clarifier

The text of the book of Nehemiah does not give any details regarding the cultivation of the vision. It is possible that God gave the vision directly to Nehemiah, which would have considerably shortened the process. Nevertheless, he was faithful in communicating and clarifying the dream, as he expressed it in chapter 2 when he appeared before both the king in Susa and the remnant in Jerusalem.

People of Influence

Birthing the vision begins with the visionary leader. It takes a visionary to develop a vision. However, with few exceptions, he must not do it alone. It is imperative that he involve others, people of influence, in the process. But who are these people of influence and what role do they play in the envisioning process?

Their Identification

These people whom I call people of influence are those who make up the leadership team. They are leaders and therefore influential people in the vision community. Fred Smith refers to them as "driving wheels" and declares their importance when he writes:

> There's a difference between people who provide the momentum in a group and those who go along for the ride. Wise leaders know that if they get the driving wheels committed, they will bring the others along. Without the commitment of the driving wheels, the organization moves unsteadily.[12]

Smith is correct. It is most important that these leaders comprehend and fully commit themselves to the vision. They need to get their fingerprints all over the vision to gain comprehension and ultimately ownership of it. This is accomplished by including them in the envisioning process. When they feel as though they have been a part of the process, and their thoughts and ideas are accurately represented in the vision, then they are more apt to commit strongly to the vision.

In the church the driving wheels are people of influence who are found at different levels of leadership. Some may be on the staff while others are on the church's board(s). Some are involved in other areas of the ministry from teaching a class of adults to serving in the nursery. Women as well as men and youth as well as adults can be driving wheels. I suggest that representatives from each of these groups be included in the envisioning process.

Their Function

The function of these people of influence in birthing the vision is fourfold.

COOPERATION

First, people of influence must cooperate with and follow the leadership of the visionary point person. It is imperative that they recognize his gifts and abilities in this area and trust his leadership in the process. They, as well as he, must avoid at all costs any power plays, special interests, and private agendas. These destructive practices have no place in the creation of a vision.

CONTRIBUTION

Second, these leaders must be a part of the process. The ability to aid in birthing the vision will vary from person to person depending on such factors as whether they are intuitive or sensing types and their other God-given gifts and abilities. Obviously some will make a greater contribution than others. It is most important that this be recognized and that different individuals contribute in proportion to their abilities.

One area where these leaders may prove indispensable is in the supply of information that is vital to the formation of the dream. For instance, they may have a better grasp of the needs, values, and dreams of the ministry community than does the ministry leader, especially if he or she is new to the area. And often they are more familiar with the culture and demographics of the ministry area. Wise leaders listen to their people, especially to the people of influence.

I suggest that ministry leaders meet regularly with their leadership and gather as much information from them as time will permit. Some individuals may be given areas to investigate and research. In light of their time and their God-given abilities, ministry leaders will take this information and use their gifts to formulate the vision statement. Then they will take this back to the team and ask them to add to, change, or delete what the leaders have produced. The vision statement may require a few changes, and the team will feel ownership by virtue of having gone through the process together.

My experience suggests that visionary point people take responsibility for writing the statement and even the initial draft of the vision statement, taking all the above information into account. Then they take that vision document and run it by their people, asking for any suggestions and input. Once they have this, they work it into the initial statement and then bring it back to their people again—preferably all together—for any further input.

SUPPORT

Third, the leadership team must rally in support of the vision. This involves far more than a simple vote in favor of the dream. They must get behind the effort, owning it with enthusiastic support backed up by personal commitment as manifest through individual involvement. If leaders cannot support the vision, then they need to find a new ministry organization with a vision they can support.

COMMUNICATION

Finally, the people of influence need to be involved in casting the vision. This is not the exclusive role of the ministry leader. The ministry community needs to hear the vision in many different ways from as many different sources as possible. One way a leadership team may serve the organization is by ministering in small groups to the individuals who make up the ministry community. This provides an ideal opportunity to communicate the dream to people on a more personal basis. The goal is that the ministry community also becomes the vision community.

THE CONTRIBUTION OF PEOPLE OF INFLUENCE

- Cooperation
- Contribution
- Support
- Communication

So far we have looked at the primary participants who are a vital part of the envisioning process. Next we turn our attention to the process itself.

QUESTIONS FOR REFLECTION AND DISCUSSION

1. If you are the senior pastor or point person in your ministry, are you a visionary? If yes, how do you know? If no, how do you know? Have you ever taken the *Myers-Briggs Type Indicator* or the *Kiersey Temperament Sorter*? What did they tell you?

2. If the point person is a visionary, what effect might this have on the ministry? If this person is not a visionary, what effect might this have? What problems might this present?

3. If you are the point person on your team and you are not a visionary, what should you do? How might you catch and communicate a vision? When or under what circumstances, if any, should you step down?

4. Who on your staff is a visionary? Are there any visionaries on the ministry's board? If so, who? If not, how might this affect the ministry and the leadership of the pastor?

5. Who are the ministry's driving wheels or people of influence? Who among them are visionaries?

4

THE VISION PROCESS

Giving Birth to Your Vision, Part 2

If the lead or senior pastor is responsible for the development of the vision, what is he supposed to do? How does the team develop a vision? Is there a process? If so, what is it?

As already noted, birthing a vision has much in common with birthing a child. First, you must concern yourself with the right personnel. If you begin with the wrong vision personnel, chances are good that you will not make it to the vision process before the entire effort aborts. If you do make it that far, the child at best will suffer birth defects.

But it is not enough to have the right personnel in place. The process is critical to the product as well. The right people going through the wrong process spells disaster. Here are the questions to be answered: How do you develop the vision? How can you custom design a unique vision for your ministry? This chapter will answer these questions by examining the vision birthing process, which consists of three stages: conception, development, and birth.

The Conception of a Dream

The birth process, whether it involves a child or a vision, begins at conception. The conception stage of a vision has at least two crucial phases: initiation and expansion. The end result of this stage is a dream that eventually leads to the vision.

The Initiation Phase

Often the dream is initiated when the dreamer either recognizes untapped opportunities or becomes dissatisfied with the status quo. Both provide fertile soil for the visionary mind.

UNTAPPED OPPORTUNITIES

Most visionaries are quick to recognize untapped opportunities. As I said earlier, they have the uncanny ability to see things that other people miss. They can drive through the inner city and see disciples where others see only poor, lost people. They see places for potential Bible studies, even churches, where others see only apartments. As they drive through their ministry communities, they see public and private schools, colleges and universities, and military bases as potential mission fields located in the very backyard of their church.

The apostle Paul was such a person. When he and Silas arrived in the city of Berea after a bad experience in Thessalonica, according to Acts 17:11, he was quick to recognize that the people in Berea were different from those in Thessalonica. The Bereans were people of integrity and were eager to know the Scriptures. This spelled opportunity for Paul, and he was quick to recognize and tap this opportunity by leading many of the Bereans to Christ, which was not possible with the people of Thessalonica. Because the Bereans were willing to examine the Scriptures, the opportunity was there. Certain Jews in Thessalonica, though, were too antagonistic toward his ministry and were not interested in the Scriptures, which meant there was no opportunity to tap.

DISSATISFACTION WITH THE STATUS QUO

Many leaders conceive a dream when they have a deep dissatisfaction with what is and a deep, pressing desire for what they know could be. Few visionary leaders are satisfied with the status quo, which for them equates to maintaining ministry mediocrity. And *mediocrity* is a word not found in their dictionaries.

As a result, they are rather easy to spot in any organization, as they challenge the status quo. They quickly discover the organization's restrictive traditions and begin to question them by periodically asking, "Why are we doing what we are doing?" Naturally, they are given such unacceptable responses as, "We've always done it that way."

Obviously this tendency to challenge what is can get visionary leaders into trouble. On the one hand it can benefit a ministry by helping it to move forward; on the other hand it can alienate people in the process. Regardless of visionary leaders' approaches to challenging the status quo, whether gentle or too abrasive, they will encounter resistance along the way. People who are less visionary and used to longstanding, restrictive traditions in their ministry organization may not understand the visionary mind-set. Challenging old ways means change, sometimes massive change, and that is the mentality of the visionary. But rather than see the potential benefits that change can bring to an organization, some feel threatened and may turn on the visionary leader.

A tool that has proved most helpful in determining one's attitude toward the status quo is the *Personal Profile* produced by the Carlson Learning Company. The profile focuses on four basic temperaments represented by the four letters *DISC*. The D stands for dominance, the I for influence, the S for steadiness, and the C for compliance. Those who fall under the first two temperaments (D and I) usually prefer to challenge the status quo, while those who fall under the last two (S and C) prefer to work with the status quo. We must also keep in mind that there are exceptions.[1] The final judge of a person's visionary capacities is the individual. However, this tool can be very helpful and can be obtained at minimal cost from most area counseling organizations or professional business consultants.[2] The advantages of this tool are that it does not take a lot of time and is self-interpretive, so it does not require professional interpretation.

I have said that visionary leaders have much difficulty with the status quo. This is primarily because in almost every situation they have an unusual ability to see critical unmet needs, shortcomings, and deficiencies in the system. Things appear to them as broken and in need of repair. They cringe when they hear, "If it ain't broke, don't fix it." To them, if you look hard enough, every organization, no matter how innovative or close to the cutting edge, has something in need of repair. There are no perfect people, and people make up ministry organizations; therefore there are no perfect organizations.

Nehemiah had difficulty with the status quo. He had inquired of Hanani and those from Judah concerning the Jews there who had escaped the Babylonian captivity. When he heard that they were in "great distress and reproach" and the wall of Jerusalem was broken down (Neh. 1:2–3), his heart was grieved, and he wept and mourned for days. Perhaps we can understand his grief best by realizing that Jerusalem was the place God had chosen for his name to dwell (v. 9). Yet this place was in a disastrous condition that Nehemiah could not tolerate. What kind of testimony was this to Israel's pagan neighbors? What kind of testimony was this to Israel's God? Nehemiah would not rest until something was done to change it.

Martin Luther King Jr. was both grieved and incensed by the general condition of black people in America. He realized that they, like the Jews in the book of Exodus, were victims of oppression and racial injustice. And it was in this very oppressive context that he conceived his dream of dignity and respect for all blacks in a free America.

These examples are most instructive. First you begin with a visionary leader such as a Nehemiah or a Martin Luther King Jr. Next you add a visionary situation involving some need or deficiency. Then you research how others in similar circumstances are dealing with these situations. If it is a church, ask, How are the newer paradigm and cutting-edge churches that God is blessing dealing with these discrepancies? The result is a profound, significant dream for the future that has the potential to empower a people to bring about cataclysmic change.

The Expansion Phase

While the dream is initiated most often by a dissatisfaction with the status quo, it expands as a result of the desire for a viable alternative: what can and must be. This signals the expansion phase.

SQUEAKY WHEELS

Visionaries are not the "squeaky wheels." People other than visionaries may express deep dissatisfaction with what is. They too may be good at spotting critical unmet needs, inconsistencies, "flies in the ministry's ointment." The problem is that these people may actually be the organization's "squeaky wheels," people within and sometimes outside the organization who constantly find fault.

These critics are most easily identified in two ways. First, many do not have any solutions for the problems they uncover and call attention to. They know something is wrong but not how to fix it. Second, there are some exceptions. There are squeaky wheels with solutions, but their solutions are characteristically out of touch with the ministry and its times. They are stalwarts of the status quo, and their ideas are heavily immersed in what is. I suspect that most of these people mean well but ultimately become more a part of the problem than a solution to the problem.

Visionary leaders are completely different from squeaky wheels. The only thing they have in common is an awareness of the flaws. However, visionaries may be characterized as opportunistic. They possess a keen sense of strategic opportunity in the midst of adversity.

They see or know of solutions for unmet needs. They acknowledge and identify the problems but usually in the same breath offer viable, compelling ideas or solutions to those problems. These solutions are concepts that push beyond what is to what can and must be. These solutions in the form of ideas make up the dream, which in turn eventually solidifies into the vision.

THE SOURCE OF THE VISION

But where do these solutions or ideas come from? Ultimately the source is God. John Haggai writes:

> Any worthy vision comes from God, whether it deals with so-called "spiritual" matters or not—and whether the person with the vision is a Christian and realizes the source of the vision or not. Worthy visions are a gift of God. James said, "Every good gift and every perfect gift is from above, and comes down from the Father of lights, with whom there is no variation or shadow of turning" (James 1:17).[3]

The visions of Moses and Nehemiah had their source in God. Moses wrote that God supplied the mission that birthed his dream from the midst of a burning bush (Exodus 3). Nehemiah acknowledged that his vision came from God when he described his dream as "what my God was putting into my mind to do for Jerusalem" (Neh. 2:12). As one goes through the vision process, somewhere between the initiation and the expansion phases, God implants the dream in the womb of the mind.

This implantation of the dream, which ultimately leads to the broader vision, may take place directly or indirectly. The above examples illustrate a more direct process. However, Warren Bennis and Burt Naus believe that the indirect process is more frequent.

> Historians tend to write about great leaders as if they possessed transcendent genius, as if they were capable of creating their visions

and sense of destiny out of some mysterious inner source. Perhaps some do, but upon closer examination it usually turns out that the vision did not originate with the leader personally but rather from others.[4]

They cite several examples in support of this view and then write the following:

> In all these cases, the leader may have been the one who chose the image from those available at the moment, articulated it, gave it form and legitimacy, and focused attention on it, but the leader only rarely was the one who conceived of the vision in the first place.[5]

In light of this, wise leaders must excel as readers and listeners and those who benefit from practical experience. In particular, they should read, listen to, and seek experience with those who think of new ideas, new images, and new paradigms. While God may directly implant the dream in the mind, more often he indirectly plants the information the leader collects from reading, listening, and practical experience as a dream in his subconscious mind. As visionary leaders view the shortcomings of a ministry and turn their attention toward a solution, this information seems to come intuitively from nowhere to form the embryo that develops into the vision.

> **THE SOURCE OF A DREAM**
>
> • Directly from God
> • Indirectly through reading, listening, and other experiences

The Development of Your Vision

During the development stage, the dream moves closer to becoming a vision. There are several methods and combinations thereof for developing your vision and your statement of it: employing the general method, expanding the mission statement, studying other vision statements, and dreaming big dreams.

Employ the General Method

The general method can be used alone or in combination with the others that follow. It consists of six steps.

STEP 1: ENVISIONING PRAYER

The first step in the general method of developing a vision is envisioning prayer. It may seem strange to bring up prayer at this point in the process. Should not the leader pray about the envisioning process much earlier than the development stage? The answer is yes. It is essential to bathe the entire process in prayer, but sometimes leaders are not aware that they are in the conception stage. It happens before they know it. All they realize is that the ministry situation has unmet needs or provides unusual opportunities, and thoughts of solutions or exciting possibilities for those opportunities have begun to synthesize in their minds. While catalytic leaders constantly pray at any time in a broad, general way for vision, now they have something specific, a dream in particular, to pray about.

I call this envisioning prayer. It is not prayer for a ministry organization in general; rather, it specifically concerns the ministry vision. This prayer is for such specific things as vision wisdom and insight, the vision community, and visionary leadership.

This envisioning prayer is intentional. It must not be a haphazard, spur-of-the-moment kind of thing. Instead, visionary leaders set aside regular times for envisioning prayer. They pray by themselves, with other leaders, and with those who make up the vision community. This sends to all others involved in the ministry process a clear message of the importance of the vision.

Jesus's own prayer life is instructive at this point. It would appear, according to Mark 1:35, that he practiced the discipline of awaking early in the morning and going to a solitary place where he could pray without interruption. While the text does not say how long Jesus prayed, it seems that visionary leaders should set aside an entire day once a month or once a quarter to get away early to a solitary place for a time of worship and prayer. It is imperative that this time include intentional prayer for and meditation on their personal and institutional visions.

As leaders practice intentional, envisioning prayer in combination with continued exposure to other visionary leaders, ideas will continue to pop into their minds and be added to their dreams. Apparently this very process was taking place in Nehemiah's head as he prayed an envisioning prayer (Neh. 1:4–11). As soon as he heard about the desperate situation in Jerusalem, he fell to his knees in prayer. God brought the vision and possibly a strategy to implement that vision to his mind. At the end of his prayer he asked God to grant him success with Artaxerxes (v. 11). Nehemiah's prayer began with the situation in Jerusalem and finished with an initial strategy in place: to appear before King Artaxerxes. These acted as prayer "bookends," between which God gave Nehemiah his vision for the remnant in Jerusalem.

STEP 2: THINKING BIG

The second step in the development of the vision is to think big. Small visions do not motivate. Someone has said, "Make no small plans, for they have not the power to stir the souls of men." Indeed, most successful vision statements are big vision statements. Several examples throughout history bear this out.

Some Who Dared to Think Big

Jesus Christ challenged a small band of disciples to reach the entire world with the gospel. When you examine the various texts on the Great Commission, you realize he was an individual of no small vision. He was a visionary par excellence.

In both Matthew 28:19 and Luke 24:47 Jesus designates whom the disciples are to reach with the gospel. They are commissioned to pursue not just a few Palestinian locals but the nations. Specifically in Matthew 28:19 they are told to "make disciples of all the nations." In Luke 24:47 they are told to preach repentance for the forgiveness of sins to "all the nations."

In Mark 16:15 and Acts 1:8 Jesus determines where the disciples are to go with the gospel. They are to go into "all the world," and they are to witness not only in their immediate community but also "in Jerusalem, and in all Judea and Samaria, and even to the remotest part of the earth."

The size of his vision is even more amazing in light of the twelve men whom he chose to accomplish the vision. Peter, Andrew, James, and John were local professional fishermen. Matthew was a despised tax collector. Why did the Savior choose them? How could a few provincial locals catch the vision for the entire world? Had they ever ventured to think outside the confines of their own community? Before it was all over, the Twelve had been reduced to eleven with the death of Judas. Yet this did not daunt the Savior, and after he returned to the Father, these same men caught and began the task of implementing his dream, which has spread across the world. In fact, you and I would not be Christians today if it had not been for them.

In his doxology in Ephesians 3 Paul challenges the Christian community at Ephesus and all who make up the church of Jesus Christ to pray and think big. Beginning in verse 14 Paul concludes the first three chapters of the book with a doxology that stretches to verse 21. In verse 20 he states, "Now to Him who is able to do far more abundantly beyond all that we ask or think, according to the power that works within us." This contains the subtle implication that we do not ask big enough things of God and we do not have big enough thoughts. In the preceding verses Paul explains that God accomplishes these things not through us but through the power that works within us, which is a reference to the Holy Spirit.

I find it interesting that even as far back as the first century AD God's community of faith had to be challenged or at least reminded to pray and think big. But this is critical if a ministry community is to be transformed into a vision community. I have observed that most people who make up a ministry community tend not to think beyond their own immediate world. Perhaps they become too caught up in the mundane affairs of everyday life. But in contrast, God seems to expect things that would appear to most people to be impossible. Consequently God raises up visionary leaders like Paul to challenge us to think big, because we have a big God who is more than able to accomplish big things through us in this big world.

Martin Luther dared to dream big dreams for God. He came to faith in Jesus Christ while a priest in the Roman Catholic Church. In light of his conversion and in contrast to the teachings of the church, he began to see the need for other viable, biblical teachings. The only problem was that in those days there was no alternative. The Catholic Church was considered to be the only teacher of one biblical truth. To consider something else was heresy and a risk to one's life. Yet his vision excited Luther and drove him on, and God used it to help fuel the Reformation.

Henry Ford had an incredibly large dream. He envisioned an affordable automobile for every family at a time when automobiles were only luxurious novelties. The average person traveled by foot, horse, train, or boat. People in his day were at first skeptical of his dream, but Ford's development of the assembly line and mass production of automobiles changed forever world manufacturing and the American way of life.

Martin Luther King Jr. envisioned not just his own freedom but that of all black Americans. He was born and raised at a time in America when some whites considered blacks to be inferior and denied them, among other things, their civil rights. Nevertheless, dauntless and at risk to his own life, King moved forward, inspired by Moses in the Old Testament, and before his assassination he saw the partial realization of his dream.

Is Your Vision Big Enough?

But how can the dreamer know if his vision is big enough? Several factors can help in assessing the size of the vision. First, the vision has to be bigger than the envisioner in the sense that it goes far beyond him and his abilities to accomplish it. If he feels that it is within his grasp to accomplish the vision, then it is probably too small and limits God. When Christians develop visions that go beyond their abilities, they are forced to bring God into the picture and begin to trust him to play the major role in realizing the vision. When this happens, in a sense, the sky becomes the limit.

Second, if the dreamer's vision is too small, her people will not feel challenged. Most people delight in being stretched in their thinking, especially in terms of their future. In general, small visions do not stretch people and motivate them to action. On the other hand, if the vision is too large, the result is discouragement. People will not view such a vision as realistic and will become frustrated and unproductive; some will drop out of the ministry.

Third, the natural tendency for most Christians is to think too small. This is Paul's point in Ephesians 3:20. The visionary leader's attitude toward risk taking may be helpful here. He needs to carefully scrutinize himself and determine if he tends to be a risk taker or not. If he does not like to take risks, then probably his vision is too small and he should try to double or triple the size of his dream. While difficult, this is what he needs at least to attempt, or he may decide the role of visionary leader does not suit him after all.

Fourth, he needs to ask, How big is my God? Most often, the size of a person's vision reflects the size of his God. People who have a big view of God have a big vision. They see him as able to accomplish big things because he is such a big God. And, of course, the opposite is true as well. People who have a small view of God have small visions. They do not see him accomplishing great things, because they have missed who he is. Here, interestingly, their vision serves as a barometer of their doctrine of God.

How to Increase the Size of Your Vision

Suppose you discover that your vision is too small. How can you grow a bigger vision? One way is to pray and ask God to increase your faith and consequently your vision (Mark 9:23–24). Second, you can surround yourself with people who think big. These could be people in the church such as business people or other pastors in the area who think big. You can also become familiar with visionaries by reading their books and articles and by listening to their messages. I would include some marketplace visionaries as well, such as Jack Welch, Ross Perot, and Joel Arthur Barker.

Another way to expand vision is to think strategically. An illustration from my own life should prove helpful. A careful study of Paul's church-planting trips in the book of Acts reveals that he and his teams did not go just anywhere but targeted strategic cities in Asia Minor, Greece, and Macedonia. Following this model, I train my potential church planters at Dallas Seminary to target strategic cities in America and abroad. For example, to plant a church in Dallas, I would target the Dallas metroplex. My strategy would be first to plant a church in a fast-growing suburban community of Dallas. Then, as the church grew, I would use it as a model and base of operations to launch other church plants in other suburban areas, the inner city, and some rural locations. I would challenge the people in these churches to target their places of work for Jesus Christ. For instance, those who work in some of the large buildings downtown could claim those buildings for the gospel. They could start prayer groups for those who are believers and evangelistic Bible studies during the lunch hour to reach those who are not.

While we might not be able to reach every person in the Dallas metroplex, our presence would be felt in the city community. If God accomplished this through Paul and his teams in Corinth, Ephesus, Berea, and other cities, why could he not accomplish the same through us in Dallas?

Step 3: Written Brainstorming

As dreamers pray envisioning prayers and think big, the next step is to begin writing their thoughts down on paper, recording the dream. I call this written brainstorming, putting on paper what God is putting on your heart. Here two important things take place: the collecting and the recording of the dream's various aspects.

This has several advantages. As God brings envisioning ideas to mind, they need to be put on paper before they are forgotten. Usually the mind works in such a way that thoughts surface in rapid-fire succession. Sometimes a brilliant idea comes from nowhere while a person drives down an expressway, listens to another, or is drifting off to sleep. Whatever the situation, there is no guarantee that the visionary will be able to recall the information later. The only wise recourse is to put this material down on paper or record it before it is forgotten.

Another advantage to written brainstorming is that it forces a person to be disciplined in his thinking as he works through the envisioning process. He should set aside regular times in his schedule to sift through his spontaneous ideas and develop the dream into the vision. He may also take time to think progressively and logically through the contents he finds in other good vision statements, as long as they do not inhibit or limit or sidetrack his own dream.

Writing also forces him to be specific. I describe this as "blowing the lint off the brain." The point is this: if an idea cannot be written down, it is far too general and vague and needs to be refined to the point where it can be written. Even then, what is first put on paper will necessarily be broad and general, but it may contain some specifics as well. The writing process captures a necessary broadness that works in tandem with a certain narrowness, both of which are necessary to arrive at a clear vision.

In written brainstorming, just as in verbal brainstorming, it is important to record all thoughts no matter how unimportant they may seem. Decisions as to their importance will be made later in the process. This is not the point at which to evaluate the information, only to collect and record it.

This means writing as many pages as necessary to record all the information that is a part of the dream. These pages may be few or numerous. The initial intuitive ideas God brings to mind will lead to a certain amount of necessary research at some point. For example, if God brings to mind a particular people group as a part of the vision, some research into the demographics and psychographics of these people will be needed, and a certain amount of this information will have to be recorded for purposes of focus.

Step 4: Determining the Contents

While creative people never cease to brainstorm, they do come to a point when it is time to organize the collected information, the fourth step in the development of the vision. This provides a skeleton later to be fleshed out with more information.

The "bones" of the skeleton are the contents found in good vision statements. What are those contents? A survey of vision statements indicates that the contents often vary, even among similar ministries such as churches. Since there are no rules that govern what may or may not go into a vision statement, this variety can be healthy; each statement reflects what is unique about a particular ministry in relation to other similar organizations.

A survey of the vision statements in the appendix shows that they may include such information as the ministry's purpose, mission, values, strategy, people, and location. Some vision statements include only a few of these details; others include many of them.

The Ministry's Purpose

Some vision documents contain a statement of purpose. This tells why the ministry exists. People need to know this, and some will want to know this. Therefore it is essential that those who are involved in a ministry or desire to plant a ministry (church planting or parachurch planting) think through and determine the purpose of that ministry. They ask and answer such questions as these: Why are we here? Why do we exist? This seems so basic that one might wonder why it should even be mentioned here. Yet in asking those involved in various ministries the *why* question, I have found that far too many do not have an answer or they answer with great difficulty. Regardless, you may want to include your answer in your vision statement.

The purpose of parachurch ministries will vary among the different organizations. Most are the same as for the church. The purpose of the church is to glorify God (Rom. 15:6; 1 Cor. 6:20). This means that what the church does in this life must cause people to value and bring honor to God. But how might the purpose statement actually be expressed in a vision statement? What would it look like? Pastor David Stevens, who planted Lakeview Community Church in Cedar Hill, Texas (a suburb of Dallas), has developed an excellent vision statement (see the appendix). In it he includes the following statement of purpose that he placed at the beginning of his vision:

> Our comprehensive purpose is to honor our Lord and Savior, Jesus Christ, by carrying out his command to make disciples of all nations (Matt. 28:19–20). Specifically, we believe God has called us to focus on reaching those in Cedar Hill and the surrounding areas who do not regularly attend any church.[6]

The Ministry's Mission

A good vision statement will contain the ministry's mission. For example, the mission of Pastor Stevens's church follows the purpose statement above. It consists of the command to make disciples of all nations.

Another example is the vision statement of Campus Crusade for Christ (now Cru). Bill Bright's mission for this parachurch ministry is found in the following quotation: "At this time and in a very definite way, God commanded me to invest my life in helping fulfill the Great Commission in this generation. I was to begin by helping to win and disciple the students of the world for Christ."[7]

Jesus Christ predetermined the mission of the church more than two thousand years ago. It is the Great Commission, that is, making disciples of all the nations (Matt. 28:19–20; Mark 16:15; Luke 26:46–47; Acts 1:8). Consequently, the vision statement of the church should creatively reflect the Great Commission. But what, more precisely, is the Great Commission? What does discipling the nations involve? Many churches wisely divide the Commission into two parts consisting of evangelism and edification, but they emphasize one at the expense of the other. I have a different view, which affects how churches and ministry organizations should try to implement the Commission in our culture in the future. According to Matthew 28:19–20 and Mark 16:15, three components make up the Commission and unfold chronologically.

The first is the intentional pursuit of lost people. This is reflected in the word *go* found at the beginning of the Commission in both Matthew 28:19 and Mark 16:15. The Savior clarifies what he means by this term in Luke 19:10 where he says, "For the Son of Man has come to seek and to save that which was lost." It is important to note that the infinitive *to save* is preceded by the infinitive *to seek*. The reason, as reflected in the context (vv. 1–10), is that the Savior's mission was first to seek out or pursue lost people and then to save them. In the context are two sections, a seeking section where the Savior pursued Zacchaeus (vv. 1–7), and a saving section where he saved the tax collector (vv. 8–9).

The second component of the Great Commission is evangelism. In Mark 16:15 Christ says, "Go into all the world and preach the gospel to all creation." A Great Commission church places a high priority on evangelism. Not only does the church in general and the members in particular actively seek lost people, but they also reach lost people.

Church growth experts indicate that a church can experience growth in one of three ways: biological, transfer, or conversion growth. Biological growth occurs when churched people have children who grow up in the church, eventually accept Christ, and continue as church members. Transfer growth takes place when people leave one church and move to another. This method of growth may or may not be beneficial depending on people's reasons for leaving their former churches. A Great Commission church grows not because it emphasizes biological or transfer growth but because of its emphasis on conversion growth. A church that does not reach the unconverted has lost its way.

The third component of the Great Commission is edification. Once the church reaches people, it does not drop them but proceeds to enfold them into the body and disciple them. This is the process of edification, which brings new believers to a Christlike, loving demeanor and lifestyle that are taught and strengthened through a combination of such critical ingredients as Bible study, fellowship, communion, worship, and prayer (Eph. 4:11–16; Acts 2:42).

The Ministry's Values

Many vision statements include in some way the ministry's values. Core values clarify what is unique about a particular ministry and drives it. They also show what the ministry will emphasize and by omission what it will not emphasize. Some of these values are biblical absolutes while others find their source in biblical truth. Vision statements for churches may include such important values as commitment to the Scriptures as God's depository of truth, excellence in leadership and ministry, relevant evangelism, an emphasis on prayer, authentic and contemporary worship, lay assessment and ministry, world missions, strong families, God's grace, social justice, full devotion to Christ, and so on. As you read through the vision statements in the appendix, you will spot some of these and many others.

The Ministry's Strategy

A fourth component found in many vision statements is the strategy the ministry will implement to accomplish its mission and vision. Again, Lakeview Community Church's vision statement contains a noteworthy strategy. It is in the paragraph that begins, "In order to accomplish this." I include here the purpose and mission statement to show how they may come together in the vision statement.

> Our comprehensive purpose is to honor our Lord and Savior, Jesus Christ, by carrying out his command to make disciples of all nations (Matt. 28:19–20). Specifically, we believe God has called us to focus on reaching those in Cedar Hill and the surrounding areas who do not regularly attend any church.
>
> In order to accomplish this, Lakeview Community Church will be an equipping center where every Christian can be developed to his or her full potential for ministry. This development will come through:
>
> a) creative, inspiring worship;
> b) teaching that is biblical and relevant to life;
> c) vital, supportive fellowship; and
> d) opportunities for outreach into the community in service and evangelism.

This strategy statement has several exemplary features. First, it refers to the church as an equipping center. This is a first-century concept found in Ephesians 4:11–12. It is the idea that the church is not only a place of ministry but also a base of ministry. However, Stevens has clothed it in fresh, descriptive language that appeals to the modern mind.

Next, it touches the felt needs of today's Christians by affirming that the church seeks their personal development. Some unchurched people caricature today's churches as sucking all the life out of a person without giving much in return. This, they contend, is done through the guise of spiritual service and is the unchurched person's excuse for not attending a church. This church's statement says you get something in return for being a part of the Lakeview community. There is value in joining with them. Their desire is to help members achieve their full potential for ministry in Christ.

Finally, the specifics of the strategy are worship, teaching, fellowship, and evangelism. It's not just any kind of worship; it is "creative, inspiring worship" that, based on Scripture, promises to relate to life as lived from Monday through Sunday. Life has a way of beating up on people, and this church says that the Bible has something to say about surviving those bouts. The fellowship is more than coffee and doughnuts before the service. Instead, the goal is vital relationships that support people who are at various stages in life. Finally, the church seeks to penetrate its community by serving the community rather than expecting the community to serve it.

The Ministry's People

Some vision statements include a reference to people. Sometimes they are the people who make up the ministry team. Most often they are the people who make up the ministry's target group. A natural question is, Whom are you attempting to reach? Lakeview Community Church has targeted those "who do not regularly attend any church" in the town of Cedar Hill, Texas. Campus Crusade (now Cru) envisions reaching the students of the world. Saddleback Valley Community Church envisions "the hundreds of thousands of residents in south Orange County." Under the leadership of Pastor Tim Armstrong, Crossroads Community Church targeted the unchurched people around Mansfield, Ohio. Some churches desire to be multicultural or multiethnic. Others target the poor and/or immigrants in particular. This should be reflected in the vision.

The Ministry's Location

A sixth component found in some vision statements is information concerning the location of the ministry. The question here is, Where will the mission and vision be realized? Most answer the question by describing their target area. This may be the immediate community. For example, the target area for Saddleback is south Orange County. For River City Community Church it is Louisville, Kentucky.

Again, Lakeview Community Church is representative: "Specifically, we believe God has called us to focus on reaching those in Cedar Hill and the surrounding areas who do not regularly attend any church." The target area may include the whole world. Lakeview Community adds, "We further intend to multiply our worldwide ministry by planting churches, by preparing our people for leadership roles in vocational ministries and parachurch groups, by sending out missionaries, and by becoming a resource center and model for Texas and the nation."

> **THE CONTENTS OF VARIOUS VISION STATEMENTS**
> - The ministry's purpose
> - The ministry's mission
> - The ministry's values
> - The ministry's strategy
> - The ministry's people
> - The ministry's location

A number of growing churches today are heavily involved in multisite and church-planting strategies to allow for greater outreach and impact in their geographical communities and beyond. This emphasis should be part of the vision statement.

In describing the place of ministry, some vision statements will cover a modest amount of demographic material. This may include the various elements that make up a community profile, one of which is statistics on the community's population, such as how many people live in the area and whether it is declining or attracting new growth.

Summary

It should be kept in mind that the majority of vision statements do not contain all of the above and some include even more material. The contents are affected by the nature of the ministry. As leaders tailor their vision statements for their particular ministries, the necessary contents will become obvious.

STEP 5: DETERMINING THE LENGTH

As I peruse the statements in the corporate world, I note that they tend to prefer shorter vision statements. In the church world, though, I find both short and long statements. Let's look at the primary advantages and disadvantages of both and some good examples of each. Then I will offer some ideas about how you can know the right length for your ministry.

Long Vision Statements

The primary advantage of a long vision statement is clarity. Since a long vision statement consists of several sentences up to several pages, it can provide more information about the church's future that will give the congregation a better picture of what is to come. The primary disadvantage of a longer statement is that it is not as memorable as a shorter statement and is more likely to be ignored or forgotten. Also, because of its length, it is harder to cast at one sitting. This would have to be done in a special, once-a-year State of the Church or Vision Night message when the emphasis is totally on vision. Another casting option would be to preach throughout the year on various parts of the vision that make up the whole. Most of the sample vision statements in the appendix are long. Note the statements of Saddleback Valley Community Church and Willow Creek, the longest of which is Willow's vision.

Short Vision Statements

The primary advantage of a short vision statement is that it is memorable. Many consist of only one sentence that can capture a congregation's attention. Also, because it is short, it is easier to cast the vision in its entirety repeatedly or at one sitting. A primary disadvantage is that a short statement lacks clarity and may be confused with a mission statement. An example is the vision statement of North Point Church. North Point's mission is to lead people into a growing relationship with Jesus Christ. And its vision is to become a church that unchurched people like to attend. Because both the mission and vision statements are short—one sentence—people can be confused as to which is which. And there is little detail, which leaves one asking for more information. Thus the vision caster will need to supply additional details when casting the vision.

The Right Length for Your Ministry

With the advantages and disadvantages in mind, how can you know which is best for your situation? One is that it simply feels right. This is most subjective but works well for some vision casters. Another perhaps better determinant is the contents of your vision, which I addressed in step 4. By taking step 4 before step 5, you will determine the length of your vision.

Of course the contents of a vision determine its length. So as you work through step 4 and find yourself wanting to add more to it, such as your mission, values, strategy, you'll find that you have to opt for a longer vision. This is okay, unless you think a short vision statement works better. By the time you arrive at step 5, you will have determined the length of your vision.

Step 6: Questioning the Dream

The last step in developing the vision is to probe the dream with constant questions. While there is no limit to the questions one can ask, here are a few musts that are definitional and make up a good vision audit.

First, is the dream clear? Can others understand it? People cannot be expected to accomplish what they do not understand. In fact, if people do not understand the vision, then, in effect, there is no vision. Obviously the best way to determine its clarity is to invite others to peruse the vision document. Ask them to explain the vision based on what is written. This adds an eye-opening objective element to what otherwise can be a subjective and blind process.

Second, is the dream exciting? When people in the ministry community hear the dream, are they inspired and excited? Often the problem with visions is that they perpetuate more of the same old thing. They do nothing more than propel the status quo into the future. The problem with this is that the status quo excites no one. Visionary leaders understand this and create exciting vision statements that propose something that few have done before. Most vision statements, though, give a new, more relevant twist to an old idea. They transform the ways things have always been done, which has an invigorating and inspiring effect on the vision audience.

Third, is the dream visual? Good visions create mental pictures. People must be able to see what the leaders see. In his book *Hey, Wait a Minute*, former pro football coach John Madden asks Vince Lombardi about the differences between good and bad coaches. Lombardi answers, "The best coaches know what the end result looks like, whether it's an offensive play, a defensive play, a defensive coverage, or just some idea of the organization. If you don't know what the end result is supposed to look like, you can't get there."[8] The same holds true for leaders and their followers. Consequently, a critical question in the envisioning process is, What do you see? Pastor Will Mancini asked this question when he developed his vision for the children's ministry at Clear Creek Community Church in Houston, Texas (see appendix).

> **DEVELOPING A VISION WITH THE GENERAL METHOD**
>
> Step 1: Envisioning prayer
> Step 2: Thinking big
> Step 3: Written brainstorming
> Step 4: Determining the contents
> Step 5: Determining the length
> Step 6: Questioning the dream

Fourth, is the dream future oriented? Vision statements are statements about the future. They create not only mental pictures but also pictures of tomorrow and what tomorrow looks like. Visions learn from the past but do not live in the past. Actually they serve as bridges from the past into the future. Dreams are preoccupied with the future and serve to project people into that future. Therefore the question should be, Is this dream preoccupied with yesterday, a rehash of the "same old same old," or is it focused on tomorrow and the exciting possibilities tomorrow holds?

Fifth, does the vision motivate those who make up the ministry to accomplish their mission? Of all the questions, perhaps the most important to the realization of the vision is this: Does it excite people and motivate them to want to pursue it? If so, you have a challenging vision. If not, you do not have a vision.

Here's a test for a good vision:

- Is it clear?
- Is it exciting?
- Can people see it (picture it)?
- Is it future focused?
- Does it motivate people to accomplish the mission?

So, how did you do? Did your vision pass the test? If you scored yourself low on any of the questions, you need to go back to that question and work on it until it does pass the test.

Expand the Mission Statement

The six steps that make up the general method for vision development are more than sufficient to help the leader develop his or her vision. Thus one may stop at this point and move on to the next chapter. However, there is a second method for developing a vision that the leader may find helpful. It includes some of the aspects of the general method above and involves the expansion of your mission statement. This assumes, of course, that you have a ministry mission statement. In the strategic thinking and acting process, I recommend that all ministries not only develop a mission statement but also develop it prior to the vision statement.[9]

The development of the vision statement begins with the mission statement and can take several approaches. One is to walk the mission statement through the six steps of the general method above. Another is to run the mission through the target group of people and the target community, if there is one, and ask, What will this mission look like as we begin to reach these people in this community? The picture that forms in your mind is your ministry vision.

Study Other Vision Statements

A third method for vision development you might want to consider is to collect and study other ministries' vision statements. In looking them over, you may discover one that grabs your attention, while the others only seem okay. You might use that one to help you with the development of yours. You could tweak it to fit your ministry situation. Ask, What is it about this vision that I like? What have the vision drafters included in this one that we should include in ours? How did they construct this vision, and how can it help us to uniquely construct ours? In developing the vision for the third church I pastored (Northwood Community Church), I took Rick Warren's vision statement and tweaked it considerably. I addressed similar areas but made it unique to my congregation's context. (See Northwood Community Church in the appendix.)

To pursue this method, you must have already collected some vision statements—the more the better. Since I have written and conducted seminars with church and parachurch organizations, I have made it a habit to collect vision statements. Several of these make up the collection in the appendix.[10] Whether or not you use this method, I would encourage you to collect vision statements, study them, and ask the questions above.

Dream Big Dreams

Another method for developing a vision is to take some time off and retreat to a quiet place, such as a lakeside cabin or a place in the mountains, where you can be creative. Once there, ask yourself,

What will the ministry look like two, five, ten, or more years from now? What do I see when I envision this ministry in the future?

This method is for highly visionary people—especially the intuitive types. They tend to carry pictures around in their mental files all the time, so this is a method tailor-made for them. As pictures and images flash in their minds, they simply record what they see.

The Birth of Your Vision

The birth of the vision occurs at that point in time when the dream becomes the vision. Perhaps the best approach to understanding the birth of a vision is to ask and answer the three important questions in this section.

When Is It a Vision?

At what point does the dream end and the vision begin? I believe that the answer to this question includes a subjective as well as an objective element. Clever words and sentences on a piece of paper do not a vision make. While they are necessary from an objective standpoint, without the subjective element, they tend to lie dormant on the page waiting for something to come along and wake them up or bring them to life.

The subjective element is found in the emotions and feelings that the visionary experiences when the vision is born. Just as emotions and feelings accompany the birth of a child, so they should accompany the birth of a vision. But what kinds of emotions and feelings does the visionary have? In my personal experience I have felt a rush or flow of excitement. In that flash of time when it all comes together, there is a sense of having arrived. It feels right or clicks in such a way as to make the dreamer feel exhilarated. There is an extreme sense of ultimate accomplishment. The visionary walks away from the process knowing that he or she has reached a milestone in the ministry if not in his or her life.

This emotional experience is important because it not only signals the birth of the vision but also provides the motivation or impetus to realize the vision in a ministry. We must be careful not to view the birth of the vision as an end in itself. Often this happens because so much work and time have gone into its development. When the vision has finally arrived, there may be a temptation to sit back, relax, and thereby cut short the envisioning process.

However, a successful birth signals not the end but the beginning of the life of a vision and the ensuing ministry. Once the vision is born, it must now be communicated, implemented, and preserved if the ministry is to grow and prosper. Otherwise you are simply a church with a vision but not a truly visionary church. What is it that initiates these events in the life of the ministry? I believe it can be that initial burst of enthusiasm coupled with the visionary leader's passion and excitement generated by the vision. While the emotions connected with the birth experience can fade over time, the memories do not. As visionary leaders cast, implement, and preserve the vision, they are reminded of the emotions surrounding its birth. The memory touches a warm place in their hearts, reminds them of how good they felt, and tends to motivate them all over again.

What Will the Vision Look Like?

How do you know when you have a vision; what does it look like? How would you know a vision if you saw it? Does it have to be several pages in length? The answer depends on a number of factors that I addressed earlier in the chapter. One is the contents of the statement. The more that is included in the document, the longer it is. The final product should be pruned to a length that includes only what is necessary to understand the vision. Otherwise, it comes across as boring and risks an early death.

Another factor that determines what the vision looks like is the people who will hear or read the statement, those for whom the vision was designed (the vision audience). Does the audience include a leadership team, potential donors, a unique target group, the public in general, or a combination of these? Determine the length and form of the statement that will most appeal to them. Those who will be involved professionally in the ministry, such as a staff, will want to know more, so the vision statement for them can be longer. Others will probably require less. When in doubt, opt for brevity—usually less is more.

Examining some of the vision statements you have collected is an additional way to answer the question, What will the new vision look like? You may want to turn to the appendix and study some of the examples there. Ask, How does our vision compare with those?

Are You Truly a Visionary Church?

At this point you must ask if you are a church that merely has a vision statement or if you truly are a visionary church. How can you know?

A truly visionary church has at least four characteristics. The first is that most of the people are excited about the vision and this motivates them to want to accomplish the church's disciple-making ministry. People will start coming to faith and growing in that faith.

METHODS FOR DEVELOPING A VISION
• Employ the general method.
• Expand the mission statement.
• Study other vision statements.
• Dream big dreams.

Second, most of the people want to be a part of the vision. They do not want to be left out, and many are willing to move in the church's new direction. This is signaled by their willingness to do whatever it takes to see the vision happen.

Third, people are talking about the vision. It has become a topic of conversation at the dinner table in homes and during the coffee break at work.

Fourth, some people will have left the church. There is no perfect church because there are no perfect people. And as long as this is the case, some people will not agree with the vision. When this happens, it is better that they leave and find another church with a vision they can believe in than stay around and try to diminish the vision of your church. If everyone is happy with the vision statement, then something is wrong with it. Good vision statements will upset some people.

QUESTIONS FOR REFLECTION AND DISCUSSION

1. Take time to think about and observe some of the potential ministry opportunities in or near your community—schools, military bases, clusters of international students, and so on. How might they be opportunities for your ministry?

2. What in your present ministry are you unsatisfied with? What really bothers you the most? Are you aware of how other ministries are dealing with these same dissatisfactions?

3. Which method for developing a vision appeals most to you? Why? Did you pick one particular method or a combination? Why?

4. Have you spent any time praying and asking God for the right vision for your ministry? Why or why not? If no, when will you start? If yes, what thoughts have popped into your head?

5. Is your tendency to think big or small? How do you explain this? What would it take for you to think bigger than what you think now?

6. Peruse the vision statements in the appendix. Do any excite you, grab your attention, or elicit some kind of emotional response? If so, which ones? How might they help you structure and develop your own vision statement?

5

IT'S A VISION!

Communicating Your Vision

As I have said, the birth of a child parallels in many ways the birth of a vision. Both are exciting, momentous occasions that demand communication of their existence to all those in the natural family or the ministry community. To birth a vision without conveying the vision would be as strange as birthing a child and not sending out birth announcements. Yet this happens in some well-meaning ministries. They develop and birth the vision but miss the importance of passing on the vision, thus frustrating themselves and risking a premature burial of the entire process. The purpose of this chapter is to explain the process for announcing the birth of the vision and to offer some practical methods for communicating the vision to the ministry community and the ministry constituency.

The Vision Casting Process

Communicating the news of a profound, significant vision for the future of a ministry involves a sender, a message, and a receiver. These are basic to any communication process and vital to the ultimate realization of any goal, mission, or vision. It is important for the leadership of a ministry organization to think through these three aspects of conveying their unique vision before they actually begin the process.

The Senders

The first step before announcing any vision is to determine who will take the responsibility for casting and conveying the vision. This should be the responsibility of everyone who is a part of the ministry—the primary leader, other leaders, and followers.

Primary Leader

As was said in chapter 3, casting the vision becomes the primary responsibility of the visionary leader who is the organization's point person and, by virtue of the position, most likely its primary spokesperson. In the parachurch organization this person is often the president or founder of the ministry. In most smaller churches this individual is the pastor, and in larger churches it is the lead or senior pastor.

Earlier I suggested that one of the primary functions of the visionary leader of any ministry is that of vision caster. This is practically assumed in most parachurch ministries; it is the leader's responsibility to travel, represent the ministry, and thus spread the vision as well as raise the necessary finances to fund the ministry.

This has not been the case in most churches. Usually the role of the pastor includes such responsibilities as teacher, preacher, evangelist, and chaplain. While most churches desire a biblical role for their pastor, the position has been affected as much by their culture as by Scripture. This can be seen in the wide variety of pastoral functions in various rural and urban settings across America. I believe that the Scriptures purposefully provide certain broad responsibilities for pastors rather than precise details. This allows them freedom and flexibility within the various cultural settings in which they minister both in America and around the world.[1]

In light of the importance of vision to the local church, I propose a new paradigm for the pastoral role that I believe will help to accomplish the Great Commission in the twenty-first century. This includes such key pastoral functions as being the primary contractor of the vision, the developer of present and potential leadership, and the primary caster of the vision.

It is this latter responsibility that concerns us here. As covered in chapter 3, the vision casting process has three parts. The first is that of vision cultivator or contractor. Here the pastor takes the responsibility of initiating and developing the ministry's vision. The second is vision caster. This involves the process of regularly holding up the vision before the ministry community. The third is vision clarifier. The primary function here is to focus the vision by regularly rethinking it and seeking to further refine it and apply it within and outside the confines of the ministry.

It is the primary responsibility of the point person in a ministry to communicate the vision, but as with the development of the vision, that person cannot do it alone. Thus it becomes imperative that he ignite others with the same vision so that they in turn achieve ownership and become vision casters as well.

Other Leaders

The other casters of the vision are the other primary and secondary leaders on the team, whether they are hired, as in some parachurch situations, or voluntary, such as the elder board in a church. In chapter 3 I called them people of influence. Their role is to follow the visionary's leadership, aid in developing the dream, rally support behind it, and pass it on to as many people as possible.

Most ministries have leaders who are at a secondary or lower level. They must not be overlooked in the casting process. They may work with people at the grassroots level and wield enough influence to either accelerate or impede the progress of the vision. The leader must meet regularly with and be part of the lives of these people as well as of those at the other levels. This is a must in any ministry, especially in churches where the majority of these faithful people are volunteers. Far too often they are asked to take some responsibility and then are abandoned to fend for themselves. The result is a high dropout rate. The role of the leader is to keep the vision before these leaders, encourage them in their walk with the Savior, and make sure they have the skills necessary to accomplish well their individual ministries.

FOLLOWERS

Finally, it is important that those who are the followers in the ministry be vision casters. These people are the employees or volunteer workers in the parachurch and the members and regular attendees in the church. They are not just the people at the grassroots level; they *are* the grass roots. They make up the audience of the visionary and are the ones who need to be convinced of the vision, for ultimately they are the people who are to be led in accomplishing the vision. The goal is not only that they catch the vision but also that they in turn cast the vision.

> **WHO CASTS THE VISION?**
> - The primary leader
> - The other leaders
> - The followers

A point person in a ministry who casts a vision for that ministry will accomplish far more for Christ's kingdom than one who has no vision or has a vision but does not cast it. When those in leadership and those at the ministry's grassroots level also work as a coalition of vision casters, the efforts of the entire ministry community are behind the efforts of the point person. In fact, this is the very strategy the Savior used in promoting the Great Commission vision among his apostles and those disciples who were a part of the early church in Acts and beyond. This kind of force is unstoppable and practically guarantees tremendous progress toward the realization of the dream.

The Message

The next step that is basic to any communication process is the determination of the message. The leader must have a message. Of course that message for the visionary leader is the vision. This may all seem rather elementary, yet too many people in positions of leadership around the world do not have a vision or do not see the need to articulate that vision.

The contents of the vision for Christian ministry have already been discussed in chapter 4. There it was determined that the essential vision for the church was established in the first century AD by Christ as the Great Commission. The vision for parachurch ministries is either the Commission or an idea subsumed under it. For example, the vision for an organization might be the evangelization of children or college students on the secular campus. The vision of another could be the writing and publication of literature that promotes discipleship and Christian maturity.

The purpose of this section is not to reiterate the contents of the vision but to present two other key factors that affect the communication of the vision message.

COMPREHENSION

The first factor in effective communication is the comprehension of the vision. The question is, Do people understand the dream? The visionary leader can capitalize on every conceivable opportunity to convey the vision, but if no one understands the vision, then as far as the ministry is concerned, there is no vision. Since we have already addressed the development and wording of the vision statement, the purpose here is to focus on the kind of context in which to present the vision most effectively for the clearest comprehension of it.

Certainly a concise, well-worded vision statement greatly affects the clarity of the vision. Often the vision statement alone may sufficiently convey the dream. But other factors will help to clarify the vision as well. One is the necessity of presenting the vision within the context of a critical deficiency or problem with the status quo. Most commonly, this is the main thing that inspired the visionary to cultivate the vision in the first place. This being the case, it would seem that communicating the vision could follow the same process: the vision becomes the solution to that deficiency or problem. This need or deficiency is first described in a speech or sermon to be followed by the vision solution.

A classic example is the presentation of the gospel as God's vision for all mankind. Most presentations begin not with the gospel but with man's need for the gospel. In Romans 3:23 Paul exposes the sinful state of mankind when he writes, "For all have sinned and fall short of the glory of God." Next, in Romans 6:23 he warns that this sin will culminate some day in spiritual death: "For the wages of sin is death, but the free gift of God is eternal life in Christ Jesus our Lord." Finally, to those who believe that their good works merit eternal favor with God, Paul writes in Ephesians 2:8–9, "For by grace you have been saved through faith; and that not of yourselves, it is the gift of God; not as a result of works, so that no one may boast." When the spiritual problem is communicated, many listeners will sense their dire need and be ready to hear the gospel or the Good News, which is the only solution to that problem.

A second classic example is God communicating his vision for his people during Nehemiah's life. In the historical context of Jerusalem's ruined walls and gates and distressed people, God raised up Nehemiah as his visionary to lead the people out of their desperate situation. In Nehemiah's first message to the people, he began by reminding them of their desperate problem, which he called their reproach. Then he invited them to join him in rebuilding the wall, which not only symbolized the vision but also was the solution to their problem (Neh. 2:17–18).

Another context in which to present the vision is that of an untapped, unexploited spiritual opportunity. Sometimes this figures in the initial development of the vision. Thus it would serve well in conveying the vision to a ministry community. In a speech or sermon the vision is presented in the context of the opportunity that motivates and catalyzes people to action. A good example is the spiritual awakening that broke out in 1989 in Mombasa, Kenya. God in his sovereignty decided to reach down and bring a considerable number of people of this region to himself. As a result, a revival of immense proportion took place, and large numbers of people came to faith in Christ. Good missions strategy says that as many people as possible should be quickly recruited and sent to such an area to help bring in the spiritual harvest.

In recruiting workers to go to Mombasa, mission representatives presented the Great Commission vision in the context of this great East African revival. This context proved most attractive for several reasons. The revival was current and the situation called for reaping the harvest, not the arduous process of sowing. Second, there was a sense of urgency. Most revivals last only a short period of time, so people needed to go before it was too late. Third, this required a short-term not a long-term personal commitment. No one needed to become a career missionary in Africa. Presenting the Great Commission vision in this context of great opportunity inspired many to join forces with those in the region to win the people for Christ.

> **TWO VISION CASTING CONTEXTS**
> 1. A critical deficiency or problem with the status quo
> 2. An untapped, unexploited spiritual opportunity

CREDIBILITY

A second key factor that affects the communication of the vision message is the credibility of the vision. The first factor asks, Do they understand it? The second asks, Do they believe in it? Any mission vision must have credibility if people are to believe in and commit themselves to it. Three elements can contribute to a credible, acceptable vision message.

The Visionary Leader's Performance

People want to know the track record of the visionary leader. This consists of such factors as God's evident blessing on a person's life and ministry, prior ministry success, strong gifts and abilities, strong communication skills, personal dedication to the cause, and a commitment to biblical values. Does the leader show extraordinary ability in any or most of these areas?

When it becomes evident that God is uniquely blessing leaders' lives and ministries, they gain extraordinary credibility in the eyes of their followers and even the general public. Sometimes God grants special favor in a person's ministry in such a way that former obstacles are removed and doors, which normally are closed, are opened.

An excellent example is in Nehemiah's vision speech when he explains, "I told them how the hand of my God had been favorable to me and also about the king's words which he had spoken to me" (Neh. 2:18). This is a reference to verses 7 and 8, where the pagan king Artaxerxes agrees to write a letter permitting Nehemiah to return to Judah and another letter asking certain individuals to supply him with the necessary resources to rebuild the gates and wall of Jerusalem.

There is no indication in the text that Nehemiah's audience knew him well. Therefore it is not surprising that he tells them of God's special hand on his work so that he might gain some credibility. This must have worked because God granted him favor again, and the people responded to his challenge and agreed to pursue the vision.

Prior ministry experience communicates credibility in Christian circles. I have observed that usually it is the fact of the experience alone and not necessarily the quality of the experience that brings credibility, especially in the selection of pastors for churches. And highly successful prior ministry experience communicates high credibility, and even a following in some cases.

The presence of strong gifts or abilities also conveys credibility, especially in the area of Christian leadership. There is a great need today for men and women with leadership expertise who can direct ministries with sustained excellence. This is because a vacuum created by the retirement of many older leaders has not yet been filled by a younger generation of leadership. Consequently, if a person has demonstrated strong leadership gifts and abilities, he or she is given high marks on the report card of credibility.

Another area that rates high is expertise as a pulpiteer, especially as the ministry increases in size. Generally people are impressed by a good communicator, that is, someone in an up-front ministry who has exposure to many people. This, coupled with the fact that currently there are not a large number of leaders known for their abilities in the pulpit, results in strong credibility.

A final element that creates trustworthiness for the vision is the personal dedication of the leader to the cause. If leaders expect their followers to commit themselves to the cause, then those leaders must demonstrate their own high commitment to the cause. Leaders accomplish this through strong personal dedication to the dream that manifests itself in self-sacrifice and personal risk taking. In most cases, the perception is that the greater the self-sacrifice or personal risk, the greater the trustworthiness of the cause.

The Content of the Vision

Another element that affects people's acceptance of the vision message is the content of the vision itself. Does it convince them of its own value? At issue is whether the vision is based on Scripture. When visionaries are able to point to a particular biblical reference in support of their dream, they catch the attention of those in the Christian community who have a high view of Scripture. Most churches and parachurch organizations are able to do this because the church's vision is the Great Commission and most parachurch visions are subsumed under that Commission.

Content credibility also depends on the relationship between the vision and the ministry community's felt needs. People award high credibility to dreams that address and offer solutions to their felt needs. Again, the Jews in Nehemiah's day were in "great distress" (Neh. 1:3) and were considered a "reproach" (2:17). Nehemiah's vision to "rebuild the wall of Jerusalem" (v. 17) was a clear, long-awaited solution to the kind of felt needs they lived with and thought about on a daily basis.

Finally, content credibility depends on the relationship between the dream and some untapped opportunity. A vision that is highly sensitive to some obvious spiritual opportunity elicits believability. An example is the current focus by some individuals and churches on reaching America's nonchurched people. The number of churches in America is declining while the number of nonchurched Americans is increasing. A survey by George Gallup revealed this and also the fact that these nonchurched people are very interested in spiritual things, and this is still the case today.[2] (They are still interested in spiritual things during the early twenty-first century but are not looking for them in the church as they did in the past.) Some visionaries have brought together the church's decline with the growth of the nonchurched and their spiritual interest to demonstrate a great opportunity to plant churches that will target and reach vast numbers of nonchurched Americans.

The Visionary Leader's Integrity

A third element that affects the people's acceptance of the vision message is the vision caster's character. Leaders who display integrity and trustworthiness are given high credibility by those within and outside the faith community. Actually the Christian community in general and the church in particular are directed to assign credibility on the basis of character. This is clearly spelled out in various passages, such as 1 Timothy 3:1–13 and Titus 1:5–9, which detail the character qualifications for Christian leadership in the church.

Character is the foundation of Christian leadership. A person's entire ministry and leadership rest on his or her character. If the character is flawed in some way, then the ministry will be flawed proportionately. This was demonstrated in the late 1980s by the fall of a number of popular television evangelists. However, in my position at a theological seminary, I observed that this time was also characterized by the fall of an unusually high number of pastors and some parachurch leaders as well. The late 1980s were difficult days for those in professional ministry positions. Sadly, much the same has continued into the twenty-first century. As might be expected, the reaction from both the Christian community

> **THREE ELEMENTS AFFECTING THE CREDIBILITY OF A VISIONARY MESSAGE**
> 1. The visionary leader's performance
> 2. Content of the vision
> 3. The visionary leader's integrity

and the secular community has been to question the credibility of Christian organizations in general. For many, the number one question concerning the leadership of any Christian organization is the integrity of its leadership.

The Receivers

The third step in conveying the vision is to consider those who will receive it. They are the ministry audience whom I divide into two groups: the ministry community and the ministry constituency. In reality, the purpose for communicating the vision is that the ministry audience own the dream and become the vision audience. When this takes place, the ministry community and constituency become the vision community and constituency. Both the terms *ministry community* and *ministry constituency* need further clarification.

The ministry community consists of all those who are directly involved in implementing the ministry vision. In a parachurch ministry they are the people who make up the ministry from the president or point person to the part-time volunteer helper. For example, in a Christian school it would include the administration, faculty, staff, student body, and parent-community supporters/helpers. In the church it includes the pastoral staff, various boards, secretarial and custodial help, and the members and regular attenders.

It is critical to the success of any ministry that these people both comprehend and own the vision. The ideal is that all the people own the vision, from the president to the mail clerk or from the pastor to the custodian. The principle is simple. The more people involved in the accomplishment of the vision, the greater the likelihood of its realization. Good dream casting wins recruits who enlarge the ministry team behind the vision. When this takes place, the ministry community becomes the empowered vision community.

The ministry constituency consists of those who are outside the ministry community. They may relate to a parachurch ministry by praying regularly for it or by contributing financially to it. They may also be recipients of the ministry in the sense that they benefit from it in some way, such as a radio audience or those on a mailing list. They may relate to a church ministry by occasional attendance, prayer, or even financial support. In any case, it is not essential that these people understand the vision and normally most do not, but a wise ministry team will do everything possible to communicate the vision to the ministry constituency so that they may become as much as possible an empowered visionary constituency. This too serves to increase even more the size of the army and its potential for accomplishing the dream.

In the above discussion, the vision audience is described as an empowered vision community and an empowered vision constituency. What does the term *empowered* mean? I do not use this term here from a strict biblical or theological perspective, as when a Christian is empowered by the Holy Spirit for ministry (Eph. 3:20), although this should be true of the people in each community. Instead, I use the term more from a leadership perspective.

In leadership, empowerment involves giving people within the organization the necessary authority and power to take responsibility for the success of their individual parts of the ministry so that the organization moves strongly toward the achievement of its vision. Thus empowerment applies more to those in the ministry community than to those in the ministry constituency but could include the latter.

Empowerment primarily affects the accomplishment of the vision once it is communicated. However, it affects the communication of the vision in that empowered people not only move to implement the vision but are good vision casters as well. Because they are sold on the vision and have strongly committed themselves to it, they become infectious in spreading the dream to other people with whom they come in contact.

> **THE MINISTRY AUDIENCE**
> - The ministry community—those who make up the ministry itself
> - The ministry constituency—those outside the ministry community

Practical Methods for Casting the Vision

The purpose of the rest of this chapter is not to elaborate on all the fine points of the communication of a concept. This can be done more effectively by consulting a text on speech communication or homiletics. Instead, this portion will feature a variety of practical methods to facilitate the casting of the ministry vision.

It should be kept in mind throughout these pages that a key to articulating the vision is to be constantly communicating the vision, using as many of these methods as possible. The problem is that most people have short memories. Most vision casters agree that it takes about one month for people to forget the vision. Consequently, casting a vision for the future is not a once-for-all event. Bill Hybels, the pastor of Willow Creek Community Church, says, "If there is anything I have learned over the years at Willow Creek, it is not to underestimate how often I need to rekindle the vision . . . to consistently reeducate people why we are on the track we are on . . . why we do things the way we do."[3] The ministry must have a number of different methods for regularly parading its dream by its people. And several of these methods may be used at the same time. In short, the rule is to repeat it over and over every day in a different way.

Some practical methods for communicating your vision are through your life, your message, electronic and nonelectronic tools, plus a number of other methods that may not have even been discovered yet.

The Visionary's Life

The leader's life communicates the vision by modeling the message. A basic requirement for a dream caster is that he first own the vision. Ownership here implies a genuine, personal commitment to the vision. This is evident when the vision excites and motivates him to the point that he finds himself constantly thinking, dreaming, and talking about it. There will be times when those closest to him will be tempted to accuse him of having a one-track mind. In some cases, the dream will keep him awake at night, because vision is like caffeine to the soul. In other words, the leader personifies the dream. He has a profound sense that he can make a difference and that the world will be a better place because of his dream. He is so convinced of his vision that not to act would seem to him a grave injustice.

An example of this kind of personal commitment to a vision is the apostle Paul. Early in his ministry his vision was to reach his people, the Jews, for Christ. He expresses his passion in Romans 10:1, where he says, "Brethren, my heart's desire and my prayer to God for them is for their salvation." His intense, personal commitment to this mission is expressed in Romans 9:3, where he states that he is willing to go so far as to be accursed, eternally separated from Christ, if it would mean the eternal salvation of his people according to the flesh.

When the leader personifies the vision, it accomplishes several things. First, he models visionary behavior for the ministry team. They watch him to see how a dream affects a person's life. His behavior answers their question—how will our dreaming the same dream affect our lives? This tends to set a new spirit among the people. They know what they can expect from him and the kind of behavior he expects from them.

Next, the leader's life brings credibility to the vision and the ministry. People, especially followers, constantly observe the leader's life for evidence of credibility. Many ask on a conscious as well as a subconscious level, Is this person qualified to lead us? Why should I follow him or her? In particular, they look to outward behavior as a chief indicator of credibility. The very thing that communicates credibility is the visionary leader's passion for the vision. When people see the emotional impact the vision has on the leader's life, they grant that leader considerable credibility. In the same manner, should the leader become disillusioned or discouraged and no longer inflamed by the vision, that leader will lose credibility with his or her constituency. A leader who has lost the vision and who tries to lead people is trying to light a fire with a wet match.

Finally, when leaders personify the vision, they motivate others to support and own the vision for themselves. A leader's enthusiasm is infectious, and others catch the vision. They believe that if the vision excites and motivates someone in the leader's position, it must be valuable and worth following. Their response, in turn, motivates still others and spreads enthusiasm throughout the entire ministry community, moving them closer to becoming a realized vision community.

In a discussion of the role of vision in successful churches, George Barna summarizes the impact of personifying the vision in the following:

> In successful churches, people were encouraged to articulate the vision through lifestyle, not just the repetition of the right words. While the degree of emphasis placed upon this type of commitment varied from church to church, all of the growing churches clearly believed that behavioral modeling was the most effective means of communicating

a concept to people. Thus, a vision that did not translate into overt action by the people was a vision that had little real support and ownership. Lacking such support and ownership, the vision—and, probably, the church—would fail to grow.[4]

The Visionary's Message

The leader's message also communicates the vision. Most often in the parachurch ministry, the message takes the form of a sermon or a speech delivered to a gathering of the entire ministry team. In the church the message usually takes the form of a sermon that is delivered Saturday evening and/or Sunday morning to the membership. The sermon or speech is a primary vehicle of the vision caster, and it is these speaking occasions that provide the visionary with an ideal opportunity to cast the vision. The question the visionary must ask on these occasions is, What is the simplest, most powerful, most exciting way to express our vision? Several important elements facilitate communicating the vision through a sermon or speech.

Understand the Audience

It is important to speak with understanding. The speaker must know and understand the audience, which most likely contains the people who make up the ministry community. This means the leader has spent enough time with the people to genuinely accept and understand them. To do less results in great difficulty in ministering to and leading those people.

The ministry community must know and believe that the leader understands their needs, dreams, hopes, and aspirations. People know that a leader cannot find solutions to their needs or turn their dreams into reality until that leader knows and understands those needs and dreams. Indeed, it is common for visions to be cast in the form of solutions to people's needs. If based on a wrong understanding of people's needs and hurts, solutions will come across as irrelevant and insipid.

The ministry community will need to hear how the vision affects or benefits them. The leader who knows and understands their needs and hopes can communicate this knowledge to them in his messages through practical illustrations and stories from their lives and his own. Next, and key to their comprehension of the vision, he must demonstrate how the vision is the solution to their problems or the realization of their hopes. For example, a message can show how too many churches in America fall far short of reaching their communities with the gospel, and it can demonstrate a need for increasing evangelistic efforts in those communities. It is critical to show that winning the community to Christ means winning the members' friends, next-door neighbors, and possibly families for the Savior as well.

Tell Stories

A second element that facilitates communicating the vision through a speech or sermon is the use of stories, a powerful tool in the hands of visionary leaders. Storytelling is a universal means of conveying information, is found in most cultures, and has been around since the creation of man. Everybody loves a good story. Consequently, the story is perhaps the most effective tool found in the vision caster's toolbox.

We can observe the effective use of storytelling in both the Old Testament and the New. For example, in 2 Samuel 12 Nathan the prophet told King David the story of how a rich man abused a poor man by taking his only lamb and using it for his personal ends. Nathan used this story to help King David realize and come to grips with the extent of his sin. The Gospels as narrative literature repeatedly communicate divine truth through telling the story of the life of Christ and his disciples. The book of Acts tells the story of what happened after the ascension of Christ and how God used the disciples in birthing and growing the early church.

Leaders who desire to communicate the dream must do so with stories. Jay Conger in *The Charismatic Leader* writes that in communicating a vision in a business setting, stories encourage more commitment than other means, such as statistics.[5] One very effective way to accomplish this in ministry is for the leader to tell his own story, his personal testimony of the impact the vision has had on his life. If the vision involves evangelism, he might tell the story of how he came to faith in Christ. The apostle Paul did this when he gave his testimony to a crowd of Jews (Acts 22) and before Agrippa (Acts 26). He addressed mostly unbelievers, and the Holy Spirit recorded this account of Paul's vision to convey it to us twenty-first-century readers.

The speaker may use a story to take us back to the early days of the founding of a successful ministry to cast the vision of that ministry. For example, Pastor Bill Hybels tells the story of the founding of Willow Creek Community Church, effectively casting Willow's vision. (See Willow's vision statement in the appendix.)

> It was evangelistic intensity that fueled the launching of this church. We used to pray in small groups in the basement of South Park Church when we were just a youth group before this church. We used to fast and pray for our friends who were outside the faith. And when we started this church we felt so strongly about it, as you know, we sold tomatoes door to door to just raise enough money to launch the first service so we could pass the gospel out, so somebody who needed to hear it would hear it and come to faith. We're going to get back to that kind of intensity.

The speaker can also tell the success stories of others. For example, there are probably other ministries similar to his that have been amazingly blessed of God. Possibly one has influenced him and his vision as mentor or model. The history of these ministries and experiences of their leaders can be obtained from someone in or near the ministry, social media, or in articles or books that recount stories about the ministry and its leader. Stories of their visions and experiences can help convey others' visions.

Personal stories of others who have come to Christ through the implementation of the vision should also be used. In demonstrating the effectiveness of friendship evangelism as a tool for accomplishing the Great Commission vision, I often tell the story of how one young housewife in our congregation developed a friendship with an unchurched neighbor who was about the same age. The neighbor was also a housewife who happened to be experiencing difficulty in her marriage. The Christian wife did a lot of patient listening and loaned her neighbor a book or two on marriage from a Christian perspective. It was only a matter of time before the neighbor accepted Christ.

Vision casters should liberally sprinkle figures of speech into their vision messages. Metaphors and similes can be highly effective. For example, earlier in this chapter I used the metaphor of trying to light a fire with a wet match. To stress the importance of giving a vision adequate time to develop, compare that process to baking a potato in an oven. You could say the dream must be carefully wrapped in the foil of creativity and baked slowly, very slowly, in the oven of time.

Figures of speech add vividness and tangibility to what otherwise could be an intangible dream. No doubt some speakers use them more easily than do others. Some people naturally think visually. They are working on a concept, and a metaphor or a simile pops intuitively into their minds. Those who find that this does not come naturally should try to train themselves to think visually by reviewing their messages or sermons and attempting to visualize their contents, translating key concepts into mental pictures, recording, and verbalizing them.

Descriptive expressions probe the imagination and create mental pictures in the listener. Pastor Bill Hybels uses such images in his message found in the appendix:

"An all-out full court press"
"To burn brighter than ever"
"To be a beacon of hope"

"The starting gun goes off"

"Turn up the evangelistic thermostat"

"Becoming contagious Christians"

SPEAK POSITIVELY

A third element that facilitates the articulation of the dream through a speech or sermon is speaking positively, not negatively. An emphasis on negatives over the years has characterized the church more than the parachurch. Some well-intentioned preachers communicate a "gloom and doom" message Sunday after Sunday. The result is a "gloom and doom" attitude on the part of the sermon audience. This emphasis on negatives has proved generally ineffective when compared with a more positive style.

There are several reasons why positive preaching inspires a profound vision. First, positive preaching is sustaining, whereas negative preaching is draining. There is energy in visionary preachers. They are dynamic people who communicate with vigor and life. The result is that God uses their messages to inspire and invigorate their followers. People hear them and realize they can accomplish what God expects because he is the power in their lives. Ultimately, they are energized to achieve their God-given potential in light of their unique divine design. Negative preaching has the opposite effect. It has a way of draining energy from its hearers. People come away convinced they cannot and probably will not ever accomplish anything of significance for God.

Positive preaching is also encouraging, whereas negative preaching is discouraging. Visionary preachers assume the role of cheerleader. Their goal is to rally people behind the dream, to enlist them for the cause of the Savior. They persuade people to look at what they can do, not what they cannot do. Positive sermons have an uplifting effect. They infuse hope and inspire followers to attempt their very best. Positive sermons acknowledge the personal worth and significance that each believer has in Christ. They also convey optimism

114

about life in general from the perspective of Romans 8:28, which says that "God causes all things to work together for good to those who love God, to those who are called according to His purpose." Constant negative preaching can take the heart out of people. After a while, they are brought down to a point where they question their own significance and the value of any service on their part for God.

By encouraging positive preaching, I do not propose never speaking out against a particular issue or ignoring sin in the lives of the people. Rather, I encourage avoiding the kind of negative preaching that seeks to motivate through false guilt, patronization, and manipulation. Avoid services every week that cause people to feel tongue-lashed or "Bible whipped," aware of their sins and shortcomings but with no understanding of God's grace and the love and forgiveness of Christ. These instruments found in the toolboxes of most negative preachers who employ them week after week ultimately serve not to edify but to demean people and the cause of Christ.

Speak with Charisma

A fourth element that aids the communication of the vision through a sermon or speech is charisma. I almost hesitate to use this term, because it has been so overused and misunderstood in both the world of leadership and theology. I do not use the term in the sense it is used today in the more experience-oriented churches, particularly those churches that strongly emphasize the presence of all the gifts of the Spirit for this day and time and the need to manifest them in the public services of the church as well as in the privacy of members' homes. Often these churches are said to be charismatic and their pastors are described as charismatic. Nor do I use the term *charisma* as if it were some mystical or mysterious experience or the effect some leaders have on people because of some mystical, exotic personality trait.

I use the term here to describe the speaker's delivery. How a speaker delivers a message may communicate as much or more than what the speaker says in the message, whether it be nonverbal or verbal. In the field of public speaking in general and homiletics in particular, charisma has to do with voice inflection, gestures, facial expressions, and eye contact. People described as charismatic are more animated in these behaviors than people not described as charismatic.

In commenting on leadership charisma, James Kouzes and Barry Posner sum up the study of social scientists who have investigated charisma as observable behavior. They discovered that in general those perceived as charismatic were characterized by the following:

> They smiled more, spoke faster, pronounced words more clearly, and moved their heads and bodies more often. They were also likely to touch others during greetings. What we call charisma can better be understood as human expressiveness.[6]

Charismatic speakers have strong personal convictions reflected in such traits as self-confidence, expertise in their field, extreme dedication to the cause, and a genuine concern for the needs of other people, which they express emphatically through their behavior, personal appearance, body language, and clothing. The result is that their messages have spark and ignite their followers.

For several years I taught a beginning homiletics course at Dallas Theological Seminary. While some of the men in the course had prior preaching experience, the majority were novices in the pulpit. Most, in time, developed the skills necessary to construct a biblical, reasonably well-developed sermon. A primary difference between those students who were effective communicators and those who were not was charisma. Those who were animated and expressive spoke with passion and moved and influenced the rest of us even in a sterile classroom environment. Those who had not yet developed charisma found that their sermons, though carefully exegeted and constructed, fell on deaf ears. They appeared as somewhat plastic, and their sermons had no punch. They left their listeners unmotivated and unmoved by the challenge of the sermon.

I believe that certain temperaments naturally display more charisma than others. However, those temperaments that display less charisma can develop some proficiency in its use in communication. Those who wish to convey significant visions would be wise to employ the use of charisma as much as possible in communicating a vision to their followers.

Speak with Conviction

A final element that enhances the communication of the dream through a verbal message is conviction. The speaker must believe strongly and genuinely in what he says. Kouzes and Posner write, "The greatest inhibitor to enlisting others in a common vision is lack of personal conviction."[7] A speaker will not communicate a vision if he is not convinced of that vision, for his message will ring with the hollow sound of insincerity. People have a way of detecting insincerity, as if they have their ears tuned for it. As stated earlier, trying to cast a vision without personal conviction is like trying to ignite a fire with a wet match.

Speakers who are convinced of their dreams are enthusiastic, committed, and motivated, with the result that they are genuine and expressive in their communication. They come across as people on a mission who speak straight from the heart. They view the podium as an ideal opportunity to expose, convince, and win hearers to their dream or point of view. Even more, they are convinced that their mission is that which is best for those in their audience. They care sincerely about and want the very best for their people, which is the realization of their vision.

A compelling vision provides direction for the message and the energy or drive to move both the speaker and the people in that direction. Visionary speakers have a way of understanding and viewing their sermon topics in the context of the overarching mission. The majority of their messages will present those topics in ways that ultimately point back to the vision. The vision casts a long shadow that encompasses and influences most if not all of the visionary speaker's messages.

At the same time, the vision supplies the visionary speaker with the energy and excitement necessary to communicate that vision powerfully and effectively. But where does the dream find its energy? I believe that at least in part the energy is derived from the conviction underlying the vision. That energy is directly proportionate to the extent to which the visionary is convinced of his dream. The stronger the conviction, the stronger will be the vision. Of course good visions are from God and are based on biblical truth, but not all leaders are equally convinced and moved by that truth. Usually men and women of strong vision have experienced the life-changing power of biblical truth at some point of difficulty in their lives and, as a result, have come away with deep, abiding convictions. It is these convictions, then, that serve to fuel a lasting fire underneath their vision.

There are numerous examples of sermons or messages that communicate vision. I encourage speakers to study them and to look specifically for examples of the five elements presented above. Vision sermons are found in Scripture. For example, in Exodus 3:4–10 God communicates to Moses his mission and vision to free his people, Israel, from Egyptian bondage and place them in a prosperous land he has prepared specifically for them. There they would be able to serve him and cast his name among the pagan nations. Moses later cast this vision as recorded in such places as Deuteronomy 8:7–9 and 11:9–12.

Many messages from the twentieth century communicate significant visions. These can be helpful because they are somewhat recent and contemporary to the culture. One that illustrates well all the above elements is that of Bill Hybels (see the appendix). A classic is the "I Have a Dream" sermon preached by Dr. Martin

Luther King Jr. on the steps of the Lincoln Memorial in Washington, DC, on August 28, 1963. While it was addressed to approximately 250,000 people who were predominantly black, it touched the conscience of the nation and moved the country forward in civil rights for minorities.

Other classic messages are presidential inaugural speeches. When a new president enters office, he communicates his vision for the country through his inaugural address. An example is President John F. Kennedy, who when he assumed the presidency in 1961 said, "And so, my fellow Americans: ask not what your country can do for you—ask what you can do for your country." He inspired a new generation to social conscience and service. Another is President Franklin Roosevelt's first inaugural speech during the Depression (1933) when he said, "The only thing we have to fear is fear itself."

> **COMMUNICATING THE VISION**
> - Understand the audience.
> - Tell stories.
> - Speak positively.
> - Speak with charisma.
> - Speak with conviction.

I encourage speakers to study and collect sermons and speeches on vision. Some can be found online. A number are available in books such as *The World's Great Speeches*, which is found online and contains numerous speeches classified into various categories according to when, where, and why they were written. While it is possible to create all one's own sermons, it is important to good dream casting to be aware of what others are saying and how they are saying it. Their contents and delivery will serve to spark thinking and provide examples and ideas for long-term vision casting.

Digital Tools

A real danger, particularly for the church, is when a sermon or speech is viewed as the only vehicle for communicating the vision. This is the reason the chapter does not end here.

Until recently the visionary leader has cast the vision primarily through a sermon or speech, which is one-way (not interactive) and word-based (not image-based). Today all that has changed. We are living in the midst of a virtual explosion of communication options, including the internet and other digital communication. Rather than teaching biblical content through colored images in stained glass or paintings or carvings in stone as in earlier centuries, now we teach the Bible with images projected by computers or other digital products on a screen. Today we have personal computers, digital video, Wi-Fi, smartphones, cloud computing, social media, and internet campuses, most of which provide affordable options that can be used to broadcast a ministry's vision. Typically the first impression people have of a church is not based on a Sunday morning visit but on a virtual visit on Facebook, a website, or online campus. People no longer need to visit your specific church location to begin to form their opinions about your congregation and catch your dream. Historically the vast majority of people in the past heard God's Word proclaimed from a pulpit in a church building. Today all we need is a smartphone to stream a message. And all this can have a profound impact on casting a ministry's vision.

This technological revolution is even making the ministry of a local church less dependent on a facility. No longer does it have to be limited to a building in a geographical location. Computing and other digital means make the universal church more universal. Any congregation can deliver any message anytime, anywhere on the planet. Currently there is talk about the entire world being wired in some way through satellite or tower coverage. All of this enhances a church's ability not only to communicate the message of Christ but also to communicate the church's vision for speaking the message.

This explosion of technology has provided a number of tools for the vision caster's tool chest. In the following I will refer to them as vehicles, venues, methods, and means for vision casting. They are simply a sampling of what is available for vision casting and are not intended to be exhaustive. In most cases the implications of each for vision casting are obvious. Thus I may or may not call attention to the vision casting capabilities of each.

WEBSITES

A website is the number one way people, especially today's Millennial generation, will find out about your church. It should contain much information about your ministry, including its mission, values, sermons/messages, service times, classes, service opportunities, staff, online giving, job postings, book reviews, articles, testimonies, different campuses if multisite, and so on. You may also include links to other helpful websites and articles. This medium is essential for communicating your vision. Websites have been around long enough that people are learning to look there to capture the ministry's vision. So do not disappoint them.

SOCIAL MEDIA

Of all the technological explosions, perhaps social media has been the biggest over a short time span. They are pervasive in nearly every sector of society. Some are comparing it in social significance to the invention and use of the printing press. Social media include tools such as Facebook, MySpace, Google+, Pinterest, Twitter, blogs, and so forth. These provide a church with a way to communicate key announcements and a place for people to connect and interact with one another during the week as well as on weekends. Most important to this book, social media provide places to clearly communicate the church's vision with the congregation, community, and the world. Not to put the vision on your church's Facebook page could be called shortsighted. Unlike a speech or sermon, social media are interactive. They are free and have proved very popular with the Millennial generation. Note that because they're interactive, people may expect a response within a reasonable amount of time.

EMAIL

Email newsletters provide a good medium with which to share information about a ministry in general and a vision in particular. However, some believe that communication by email is becoming ineffective because of the overabundance of emails people receive each day.

MOBILE APPS

Mobile apps, short for mobile applications, consist of application software designed to run on smartphones, tablet computers, and other mobile devices. Churches can create their own unique apps. They may use these apps to stream media and provide important information regarding their programs in general and their vision in particular. A church would be wise to create and regularly update a special vision app for the church itself and those people who live in its community.

TEXTING/TEXT BLASTING

Texting is a quick, efficient means to connect with people. Text blasting lets you contact your congregation or a large number of people instantly at any time. When used wisely, it provides a good means for casting your congregational dream.

PODCASTS

Podcasts are a digital medium or program for automatic download over the internet. Podcasts are simple to produce (you need only a microphone and a computer) and can be put on your website or on other services, such as iTunes, without cost to you. Sound good? Churches use them for making sermons and other training material available. And they can prove ideal for vision casting.

YOUTUBE VIDEOS

YouTube is a video-sharing website owned by Google that allows you to produce training videos and record sermons or special messages that would include your dream for your people. Users can upload, view, and share their videos, and they work universally on multiple devices with minimal hassle.

LIVE STREAMING

The audio and likely the video of your church services can be streamed live, and these services themselves communicate your vision. If evangelism is part of your vision, then it will be reflected in some way in your ministries. This is a great way to connect with and communicate your vision to people who for some reason aren't able to attend your church.

WEBINARS/WEBCASTS

Webinars, also known as webcasts, allow conferencing events to be shared with remote locations. The service allows real-time point-to-point communications as well as multicast communications from one sender to many receivers. It offers data streams of text-based messages and voice and video chat to be shared simultaneously across geographically dispersed locations. Applications for Web conferencing include meetings, training events, lectures, or short presentations from any computer. They provide ideal opportunities to communicate and explain a ministry's vision.

COMPUTER/VIDEO KIOSKS

Computer and/or video kiosks are small computer terminals that a church could place at key locations, such as in malls and stores, to communicate the congregation's presence in the community and attract unchurched people with its vision. Churches may place them within their facilities as well to display multimedia messages and information as to where a class or small group might be held.

ONLINE BULLETIN

An online bulletin can provide much information about a church and all that is happening on a timely basis along with ministry opportunities.

Nondigital Tools

Due to the popularity of digital tools, we might be tempted to ignore the number of nondigital tools that are available to cast the church's vision. The ideal is to use both, depending on your vision audience. Some nondigital tools that may serve to communicate your vision include a new members class, a newcomers class, a state of the church/ministry sermon, a printed brochure, face-to-face interactions (small groups, counseling, and so forth), print magazines, flyers, town hall meetings, "Lunch and Learn" events, retreats, mission trips, T-shirts, word of mouth, posters, banners, and vision testimonies.

The Tools Problem

In light of the current explosion of technology, keeping up with all these tools can be a problem. What's fading in popularity? What's new on the scene? I mention all the above tools—especially the electronic tools—with fear and trembling because before the ink has dried on the pages of this book, a particular tool will be out of date and new tools will appear that will make some of these, as well as me, look obsolete.

Here are five important reminders that will help you get the most out of these tools.

1. *Let the size of your church determine how many tools you use.* A large church may use more than a small church. Some recommend the use of no more than three to five tools for the small church due to the potential lack of enough people to do this well. Focus on using less and doing them extra well. In this case, less is more. For example, one church limited its use to five tools: a website, Facebook, a bulletin, an e-blast, and worship service announcements.

2. *Consider your audience.* Who are they? This would include demographics. Are they mostly older, younger, or a blend? Are

they tech savvy? What may work with a younger generation (the electronic tools above) will not necessarily work with an older generation who may prefer oral communication, such as announcements from the pulpit.

3. *Consider which are most effective for your people.* Which best serve your church and its mission in general and vision in particular? It's better not to attempt to use a tool if it won't be effective for your particular group.

4. *Remember that the medium is the message.* The media you choose for sending a message send a message themselves. Thus it's important how you communicate a message. For example, some churches still use an overhead projector to convey information. What does the use of such a tool say about the ministry in terms of being relevant and "in touch"?

5. *Since the medium is the message, make sure that someone regularly uses and updates these tools.* People expect and appreciate updated methods of communication. Having these tools but not using them is a turnoff for people. The same is true if they are not properly maintained. Remember that the use and upkeep of your tools will take time. Who will have time to make sure they are regularly updated? Will it be a part-time or full-time person? Someone—perhaps the same person who does the maintenance—will also need to monitor social media to respond to people who communicate in that way.

> PRACTICAL METHODS
> FOR CASTING A VISION
> - The visionary's life
> - The visionary's message/sermon
> - Digital tools
> - Nondigital tools

It must be kept in mind that developing and communicating the vision does not necessarily guarantee the realization of the vision. Another step has to be taken after the initial communication of the dream. This is the implementation of the dream. The next two chapters are designed to explain what is involved in this important process.

1. In every ministry the primary leader is responsible for the communication of the vision. Are you that person? If not, who is? Candidly, is the job being done? Are others in the ministry casting the vision? Why or why not?

2. Are you aware of any critical deficiencies or problems with the status quo that relate in some way to your ministry? What are they? Can you use any of these situations as a context for your vision?

3. Are there any untapped or unexploited opportunities in your community that your ministry could use as a context for casting your dream? Ask some of the people who are part of your ministry if they are aware of any opportunities.

4. Have you ever sensed God's hand of blessing on you and your ministry in a special way, such as Nehemiah experienced? List some of these occurrences.

5. How would you rate yourself as a speaker and potential vision caster? Do not be too humble. How does someone else in your ministry who has been exposed to other good speakers rate you? How about your spouse? Are you afraid to ask?

6. Who makes up your ministry community? Who makes up your ministry constituency? Can you visualize either your community or your constituency as a vision community or vision constituency?

7. Does your dream excite you? Do you talk about it often with other people who might be interested? Have you ever lain awake at night thinking about it?

8. Have you collected any good vision stories to tell? Are there any ministries similar to yours that excite you and have been obviously blessed of God? What stories can you glean from them that might be useful in casting your vision?

9. Which of the practical methods for communicating the vision listed in this chapter would work in your situation? What other practical methods popped into your mind as you read through them? Were they digital or nondigital methods? Did you write them down in the margin of the book? If you did not, go back and do it now before you forget them.

6

Overcoming Initial Inertia

Implementing Your Vision, Part 1

Assuming that a leader understands the reasons a vision is so critical to a church or parachurch ministry and has developed a clear exciting vision that motivates his or her community to want to realize that vision, the leader must ask, Where do we go from here?

The answer is that now it is time to implement the vision. But good implementation has proven to be the greatest problem in strategizing. Surveys indicate that nine out of ten organizations fail to implement properly the strategies they formulate. Therefore this chapter will begin by assessing the problem. Then it will present the solution to this problem (team building) and show how to implement that solution.

Assessing the Problem

Once the vision is developed and being communicated, the process is not over. Although it helps immensely, good dream casting by itself does not necessarily result in the implementation of the dream. There yet remains another key step in the all-important envisioning process. The vision has to be implemented. The dream must be transformed into concrete reality. If this step does not take place, then most likely the vision will remain "pie in the sky by and by," a recurring item on a board's monthly agenda.

I believe this transformational step is probably the most difficult aspect of the entire process. It is problematic for two reasons. First, it calls on the visionary leader's interpersonal skills and abilities to work well with people in the envisioning process. Some leaders have more expertise here than others. Also, this critical area is not included in most pastors' seminary curriculum. They receive little to no training in interpersonal skills.

> **TWO FACTORS THAT DETERMINE IMPLEMENTATION**
> 1. The leader's interpersonal skills and ability to work with people
> 2. The followers' ability to work together as a team

Another reason this step is difficult is that at this point a leader entrusts the vision to people of influence for its implementation. To a large degree it is then out of the visionary's hands and dependent on the commitment, aspirations, and spiritual maturity of other people. The question is, Will these other people carry the ball or fumble it? If some are not quick to see the vision or have other agendas, there will be a problem. But there is a solution to this problem. I call it team building.

Team Building

At this point, some would advise that the solution to a pastor's problem of how to implement his vision is good management; that is, he needs to develop a plan. However, this is not the solution for the simple reason that it takes people to implement any plan. While it is true that some influential people may be behind the vision, this is not enough, for it takes a team of people to implement a vision.

Far too often at this point, pastors do not yet have a full team, not enough people on the same playing field moving in the same direction. To introduce a plan now will result in a slow, frustrating death for the vision. Although some people will carry through on their planning assignments, others will do so halfheartedly or not at all. The solution to this problem, and the leader's number one priority if he is to implement the dream, is to craft a team who will own the dream. Here it is important that I pause to define what I'm talking about—what is team building. And what kind of response might a leader encounter in building a team.

Team building is the careful, patient construction of a team (two or more people) around the organizational vision for the purpose of implementing the vision. When a new leader with his vision comes into an established ministry, such as a church, not everyone will be on his team. Some will be on the pastor's team either because they like him or because they are naturally attracted to his vision, but there will be some of the board as well as some of the people who will need more time before they can join the team. They are by temperament slower decision makers. They want time to think through the vision and its implications for them and the ministry. This should be acceptable unless it turns into procrastination. Most likely, those individuals will own the vision and join the team in time. When this happens, the team will begin to move toward the vision's implementation.

There will be some people, possibly a large number, who never own the vision. If the number is large, the visionary leader is in trouble and will have to make a critical choice about remaining and pushing the vision—which could result in a split in the organization—backing off and letting the vision die a slow death, or moving to another ministry.

In the more common situation, where only one or two individuals will not embrace the dream with the rest, it is best to move to implement the vision without their support. The question for them is whether they will go along with the rest or resist the effort to implement the vision. If the answer is the latter, they will need to be dealt with accordingly. Regardless of their response, you can expect them eventually to pack their bags and leave the church.

The Role of Leadership in Team Building

Successfully building a team depends primarily on the visionary's leadership skills more than on management skills. Contrary to popular opinion, leadership and management are two separate but complementary systems of action. John Kotter summarizes well the difference between the two. He writes that leadership is about coping with change, while management is about coping with complexity.[1] This chapter and the next focus on change.

According to Kotter, leadership copes with change through three steps. First, it establishes the direction where a group of people should go, using vision and strategy to chart a clear course through the fog of change. This corresponds with what I have called the development of the vision. Next, leadership communicates that vision to its people and secures their commitment to move in that direction, which Kotter calls alignment. This corresponds roughly with what I call the casting of the vision. Team building begins at this point as attempts are made to secure a commitment from people to move with the vision. Finally, leadership energizes people so they will be able to overcome the various obstacles that are sure to surface along the way. Kotter calls this motivation and inspiration.[2] In my process, all of this comes under team building.

HOW LEADERSHIP COPES WITH COMPLEXITY

- Planning and budgeting
- Organizing and staffing
- Controlling and problem solving

In contrast to leadership, Kotter writes that management copes with complexity in three ways. The first is planning and budgeting, which establish goals and the steps necessary to reach those goals and include allocating the funds to make it happen. The second is organizing and staffing, which mean establishing a structure and a set of jobs to accomplish the plan. The third is controlling or monitoring the progress of the plan and solving problems as they surface.[3]

The Two Agendas of Team Building

The visionary leader puts on the helmet of leadership and functions as a player-coach. The kind of team building that implements the vision and wins the game has two agendas. The first agenda is to acquire a commitment from potential players with different interests, backgrounds, ideas, needs, gifts, and abilities to join others who are already on the field and to move together as a team toward the same goal. This can be a pastor's most immediate problem. Some of the people on their board may not have joined the team on the field. They are still sitting on the sidelines trying to understand the pastor's direction and wondering if they should play the game his way. Consequently, the pastor may have to overcome some initial inertia. This chapter will focus on this agenda.

The second agenda is to help these same people, once they are moving down the field toward the same goal, to overcome various obstacles that are sure to surface as the game progresses. A common fact of life is that nothing progresses as expected. In football, for example, the quarterback may be injured or the team may run out of downs and face a critical fourth down situation with only inches to go. Since the fall, life has been full of glitches. What is true of football is true of life in general. The next chapter will focus on this second agenda.

Now that we understand the role of leadership and two agendas of team building, we must ask, What could help the typical pastor?

> **THE TWO AGENDAS OF TEAM BUILDING**
> 1. To acquire a commitment from all players to join the team and move down the field together
> 2. To help these players overcome obstacles that are sure to surface

How can he craft a team? What practical steps might he take? In the church or parachurch, how does the coach acquire the best players? He must first overcome the initial inertia that surfaces in every situation including ministry. There are at least three steps to do so.

STEP 1: REALIZING THE IMPORTANCE OF THE TEAM

Leaders must not pattern themselves after the Lone Ranger. Remember, even the Lone Ranger had Tonto. Ultimately, no team means no dream. The reason we quickly forget this is because the people who make up the team have most often taken a backseat to the visionary, which is necessary if he or she is to exercise the leadership necessary to realize the common dream. When we hear of successful ministries, it is usually the leader, not the team, who gets most of the credit.

The team concept is not new to any student of the Scriptures—New Testament ministry is team ministry. This principle is well illustrated in the ministries of both the Savior and the apostle Paul. It should be kept in mind that their teams were largely responsible for initiating the spread of Christianity around the world and that twenty centuries later our faith in Christ can be traced to their teamwork.

Jesus Valued the Team

Jesus Christ as deity has all authority and power in heaven and on earth (Matt. 28:18). This great truth was regularly celebrated in the Old Testament when the various writers and prophets reminded the people of Israel that their God was the One who created the heavens and earth and all that is in them. In the Gospels Jesus exercised his awesome power to perform various miracles, such as healing the sick and raising the dead. It is important to note that he did not need his band of unimpressive, common laborers to realize his mission, for he could have accomplished it on the spot with only a command from his lips (26:53). It could have been a sacred solo performance. Yet instead of doing it alone, he chose to work through them. Later, the

Gospels record, he did much the same when he appointed and sent out seventy others in addition to the apostles (Luke 10).

Paul Valued the Team

The apostle Paul did not, of course, have the same power and authority as the Son of God, and he chose not to attempt the Great Commission vision alone but decided to work through a team effort. Prior to his first church-planting journey, the team consisted of Barnabas and Paul (Acts 11:22–30). Then, on the first church-planting trip, they added Mark to the team (13:2, 3, 5). On the second trip, he added Silas (15:40), Timothy (16:1–3), Luke (Acts 16), and others (Acts 18). Finally, on the third trip, additional people were either added to the team or used to form new teams. Thus in Acts 19 and 20, such names appear as Erastus, Gaius, Aristarchus, Sopater, Secundus, and Tychicus. In addition, Paul, in some of his letters, identifies various individuals who may very well have been important members of his team, such as those mentioned in Romans 16:21–23.

In light of the ministries of Jesus and Paul, there can be little doubt that New Testament ministry was team ministry. Some leaders have proved slow to learn this basic lesson. They become so motivated by the vision that they run far out ahead of their team and attempt to implement it on their own. They function as a team of one.

Step 2: Recruiting the Team

Whenever leaders decide to recruit a team to implement the dream, they must ask and answer two questions: Who will make up the team? How will we enlist these people?

Who will be on the team? The answer depends on the nature of the ministry organization and who is in strategic positions to influence, either positively or negatively, the implementation of the dream.

If the organization is parachurch, then most likely the team will consist of those who make up the immediate ministry community, such as the various staff and personnel. If the organization is a local church, then the team will consist of those who are on the ministry staff plus any leadership boards.

However, in both church and parachurch ministries, this should be viewed only as a beginning. It is hoped that these people, in turn, will recruit all others who in some way can create coalitions that both understand and are committed to the dream's realization. Therefore recruitment is everyone's business. The goal is to recruit recruiters and to enlist enlisters. The hope ultimately is to reach anyone who is in a position either to help or to stymie the implementation of the dream.

How will they be recruited? The primary recruitment tool is the vision or dream itself. Constantly conveying a vision that will excite and meet the audience's basic spiritual values, needs, and aspirations will recruit recruits. It is akin to offering a thirsty person a cold drink of water on a hot summer day. Most people find it hard to resist a vision that proposes to deliver in these areas of their lives.

This recruitment tool can be used in both planted and established ministries. The advantage of using vision casting as a vehicle for recruitment in a new ministry start is the leader's greater capacity to know who is committed to the vision from the very beginning. Usually those who are not committed to the vision will not stay around; they vote with their feet.

In established ministries where there may not be a vision, dream casting will bring to the surface those who are thirsty and those who are not. The next step, building the team, should help to win over those who are not thirsty.

Again, the desire is that once these people have enlisted, they, in turn, will enlist others. This is well illustrated by the recruitment that took place among the apostles. In John 1:38–40 the Savior invited Andrew and another disciple to come and stay with him for a day. Next, Andrew recruited his brother Peter (vv. 41–42). Then Jesus recruited Philip (v. 43). Then Philip found and recruited Nathanael (vv. 45–51). Hopefully this recruitment process will continue throughout the life of the ministry, especially in the church. There will always be a need for team members. That is another reason for continually keeping the vision before the people's eyes.

STEP 3: CRAFTING THE TEAM

Once visionary leaders recognize the importance of the team to their ministry and then recruit the best team possible, they are finally ready to craft their team into a unit that can accomplish the first agenda. This is step three. The rest of this chapter consists of two sections that describe how to build or craft a team. The first discusses the critical elements of commitment and cooperation in constructing a team and how the one affects the other. The second shows how to catalyze the kind of commitment in people that builds strong teams.

The Elements of Commitment and Cooperation

Team building cannot be accomplished without two key ingredients: commitment and cooperation. Often a pastor will discover that some of his leaders are committed and cooperating and some are not.

Commitment

Any good coach will affirm the fact that it takes commitment, lots of commitment, to play the game of football. Most who watch a college or professional game on television are not always aware of this, but behind every weekend performance has been an entire week of long, sometimes agonizing practices, not to mention the fact that some players are coping with various nagging injuries.

In most cases the amount of success athletes experience on the field can be measured by the degree of their commitment to the total process both on and off the field. John Kotter says that a key ingredient of leadership is getting the team to understand the

137

vision and be committed to its achievement.[4] The degree to which the ministry leadership team accomplishes their vision depends on their willingness to do whatever it takes to get the job done. Without this commitment, the entire envisioning process comes to a frustrating halt.

Cooperation

Any good football coach will agree that in addition to commitment, it takes lots of cooperation to win at the game of football. If an offensive lineman decides that he does not want to block for the quarterback when he drops back to pass or for a back when he runs with the ball, the result could be disaster. The implementation of a dream, like the game of football, depends on mutual cooperation among all the players in the game. The degree to which the team wins or loses depends on their willingness to work together.

At the same time most people acknowledge that cooperation is not easy. However, people who work together under the same dream are more inclined toward ensuring one another's success. When people are free to use their God-given talents and abilities, mutual cooperation replaces mutual competition—and brings success. The success of one member of the team means the success of all the members of the team. In their book *The Leadership Challenge*, James Kouzes and Barry Posner write:

> Fostering collaboration is not just a nice idea. It is the key that leaders use to unlock the energies and talents available in their organizations. . . . Leaders realize that the key to doing well is not in competition or in overcoming others but in gaining their cooperation.[5]

Commitment affects cooperation. Whether the sport of football or the field of ministry, cooperation is the fruit of commitment. The degree of cooperation is directly proportional to the degree of commitment. The higher the commitment to the dream, the higher will be the cooperation to achieve that dream. Therefore the leader who is able to enlist the commitment of his people will most likely also gain the cooperation of his people, and the result is strong teams. In a sense, then, the issue is commitment. But how might he win a heart commitment from his entire team?

Catalyzing Commitment in a Potential Team

Leaders can build commitment in their people in four ways: helping them discover that they need one another, creating a climate of trust and vulnerability, developing a sense of community spirit, and maintaining clear lines of communication.

Helping People Discover They Need One Another

When a well-designed vision articulates an exciting, dynamic picture of the future and addresses people's spiritual needs, then, when people are recruited for the team, they are willing to commit themselves to implement that team.

As I have said, commitment cultivated by the vision affects cooperation. A problem that plagues team building is the mutual rivalry that sometimes erupts between team members who have different gifts and abilities. Most people believe that other people are just like them, that they think and see the world through the same pair of glasses and share the same talents and passions. Consequently, when others behave or think differently, people become critical of them, which fosters competition instead of cooperation. The apostle Paul addresses this in 1 Corinthians 12:17–20:

> If the whole body were an eye, where would the hearing be? If the whole were hearing, where would the sense of smell be? But now God has placed the members, each one of them, in the body, just as

He desired. If they were all one member, where would the body be? But now there are many members, but one body.

However, when all share a deep commitment to the same dream, they begin to realize that it takes people with different but complementary gifts, talents, and abilities to accomplish that dream. Each person on the team realizes that he or she needs the other persons if anything of significance is to be accomplished for the Savior, and members value and appreciate how God has designed each one differently so that all can, in fact, realize what they desire. The potential for destructive competition is eliminated and replaced by mutual cooperation. Team members will then acknowledge that without one another success will not happen.

Creating a Climate of Trust and Vulnerability

People who implicitly trust one another work well together. They foster mutual cooperation toward reaching group goals. Those who do not trust one another accomplish little, which signals an early funeral for most teams.

Lack of trust was the major factor in the dissolution of the Paul-Barnabas team in Acts 15:37–40. At issue was the credibility of a former team member, John Mark, who, according to verse 38, had deserted them in a prior ministry situation in Pamphylia. In light of this breach of confidence, Paul believed that John Mark could not be trusted in future ministry situations. Barnabas disagreed and believed they should give the man another chance. Trust was such an important issue to these men that they decided to part company, form separate teams, and go their separate ways.

There are several ways to cultivate a climate of trust. To begin, the leader must set the example. If he expects people on the team to trust one another, then it is imperative that he trust them. Perhaps this was Barnabas's thinking in giving John Mark a second chance. A good rule of thumb is to trust people until they give you a reason not to. This may have been the factor in Paul's rejection of John Mark.

This does not mean that people always have to agree with one another. For example, there is not a person on the faculty at Dallas Seminary whom I do not trust. In fact, I would trust any faculty person with my life. I suspect that they feel the same way toward me. At the same time, this does not mean that we always agree. Our mutual trust, however, creates an environment in which we as a faculty team can resolve our differences, love one another, and accomplish our vision as an institution.

Another way to model and cultivate trust is to delegate responsibilities. We see this in the example of the Savior when he delegated ministry to the disciples, as in Matthew 10, and to the seventy in Luke 10.

A leader cultivates trust when he is open and thus vulnerable to people on the team. His willingness to share his deepest fears or greatest shortcomings with others communicates that he trusts them and grants them a certain degree of integrity. They are thereby encouraged to be similarly open and honest.

> **FOUR WAYS LEADERS DEVELOP A CLIMATE OF TRUST**
> 1. They trust people.
> 2. They delegate ministry responsibilities.
> 3. They model openness and vulnerability.
> 4. They encourage others to participate in decision making.

Leaders also develop trust when they encourage others to participate in decision making, especially when it relates to their areas of expertise. For example, when my departmental team at Dallas Seminary meets together, one of the members may raise an issue that calls for a decision. My response is to ask what this particular member recommends we do, since this lies within his or her area of ministry expertise. Very rarely do we not follow that recommendation. This communicates loudly our faith in our colleague and his or her ability to lead and manage with sustained excellence.

Developing a Sense of Community Spirit

To encourage commitment to a team, it is essential to develop a sense that all on the team are part of the same community, imparting a sense of togetherness. This is not *my* ministry; it is *our* ministry. This is not *my* dream; it is *our* dream. Use the pronoun *we* rather than *I*, or *our* rather than *my*. Kouzes and Posner suggest this:

> *Always say we.* When thinking and talking about what you plan to accomplish and have accomplished, it is essential that you think and talk in terms of *our* goals. Your task as a leader is to help other people to reach mutual goals, not your goals. You never accomplish anything alone, so your attitude can never be "here's what I did" but rather "here's what we did." This language reinforces the belief that goals are truly collaborative, not exploitative.[6]

It is instructive to trace the use of these pronouns through the book of Acts by the various teams of Peter and John (Acts 4:20), the apostles (5:29), Paul and Barnabas (15:36), and others.

Another way to develop a sense of community or team spirit is by spending time together. This makes it possible for people to get to know one another beyond the normal daily office or monthly board routines. The better you know other people, the better you understand them and their various life circumstances. This helps you discern why they do the things they do, whether good or bad. This concept is not without excellent precedent. Jesus chose to spend time with the twelve disciples. "He appointed twelve, so that they would be with Him and that He could send them out to preach" (Mark 3:14). Those in the early church spent time together in fellowship and small groups (Acts 2:42, 46).

In a church this can be accomplished by frequent staff and/or board retreats, participation in small groups, visiting in homes, and so on. In a parachurch ministry it can happen through such events as birthday parties, socials, luncheons, and company picnics. The only limit on all the possibilities is one's imagination. Of great value in particular is mutual participation in team sporting events such as volleyball, basketball, softball, or golf. This enables people to play together in team situations that are different from those normally experienced at work or the church. The idea is that those who play together stay together.

> **TWO KEYS TO DEVELOPING A SENSE OF COMMUNITY**
> 1. Use the pronouns *we* and *our.*
> 2. Spend time together as a team.

Maintaining Clear Lines of Communication

Most individuals want to know what is going on. They want to keep abreast of what is taking place in their ministry or workplace. John Naisbitt illustrates this from the marketplace when in *Megatrends 2000* he writes:

> People want to know what is going on in their company. In the same Steelcase poll, 76 percent rated "free exchange of information among employees and departments" very important; only 35 percent said it described their office.[7]

Later in the same article, he quotes Everett Sanders, chairman of three Atlanta companies:

> "As time went on, my managers became almost as interested in all facets of the company as I was," he says. People who are kept posted, he says, feel they have a stake in the company and "work even harder when all is not going well."[8]

If people ever begin to suspect that the leader is hiding something from them, he will lose considerable credibility. Paul urges us to speak the truth in love (Eph. 4:15). Those involved in team ministries deserve to know the truth about what is taking place on the team. The key, as Paul says, is to communicate it in love.

143

It is best to communicate face-to-face. It is instructive to note that whenever there is conflict between people, Jesus urges them to get together and seek resolution (Matt. 5:23–24; 18:15–17). One-on-one communication allows people to be open, honest, and emotional if necessary without having to worry about what others will think. The advantage is that if someone has some negative information about another person that is not correct, the situation can be corrected without damaging the person's reputation.

Another way to communicate is in a group context. A leader may address the team, or several people in turn may address the team, as in Acts 15:6–21; 20:17.

Good communication that builds commitment includes the resolution of any conflicts between people who are on the same team. It goes almost without saying that people will not cooperate with those with whom there has been some kind of unresolved strife. It is common in ministry to hear horror stories about churches where board members frequently skirmish with one another or the pastor because of some unresolved conflict.

HOW TO MAINTAIN CLEAR LINES OF COMMUNICATION

- Keep your people informed.
- Communicate face-to-face.
- Communicate in a group context.
- Seek to resolve conflicts.

Both Matthew 5:23–24 and Matthew 18:15 urge that conflicts be resolved quickly at the initiative of either the offending or the offended party. The point is: Get it taken care of. The wisdom here is evident because the longer a problem goes without resolution, the worse it becomes. The importance of resolution is emphasized in Matthew 5:24, where it is given priority over worship.

Visionary leaders who work hard at building commitment and cooperation in their people will empower teams that work together toward a positive, significant dream for the future. This accomplishes the first agenda of team building. However, that same team will run headlong into various obstacles on the way toward the realization of their dream. Overcoming them is the second agenda of team building, the topic of the next chapter.

Worksheet

Evaluating Your Group

1. On a blank sheet of paper draw two horizontal lines from one side of the page to the other about one or two inches apart. Place the numerals 1 through 10 from left to right on both lines. Write *commitment* above the first line and *cooperation* above the second.

2. Rate as a whole the group you are working with in terms of their commitment to one another and to the vision. Circle the number on the appropriate line (1 is the lowest; 10 is the highest). Rate the cooperation of the team in working together and circle the number on that line.

3. In the same way rate each individual in the group, including yourself.

4. If your group scored below 5 as a whole, you need to answer several key questions.

    a. How long have you been with this ministry?

    b. Do you understand how to build a crowd into a team?

    c. Have you been with this group long enough that you should have seen some progress by now?

    d. Do these people need more time? If your answer is yes, are you being realistic?

    e. Do you see progress or growth on the part of the group as a whole or in the lives of certain individuals?

    f. Is it time to consider another ministry?

5. Did any of the individuals in the group score below 5?

    a. How many?

    b. Why do these individuals struggle with commitment and cooperation?

    c. Do you believe these individuals will grow and improve in these areas? Why or why not?

    d. Will you discuss the situation with them?

    e. What are the chances of their leaving the group?

Building a Team

1. Help people discover that they need one another.

    a. Do you feel that you have a good understanding of your group's needs, hopes, and aspirations for the future? Can you list them?

    b. Have you cast your vision in such a way that your group sees how it relates to their needs, hopes, and aspirations?

2. Create a climate of trust and vulnerability.

    a. Do you trust the people in your group, and do they trust you? Why or why not?

    b. Do you delegate responsibility to the people in the group? Why or why not?

    c. Are you vulnerable with your group? Have you ever shared your fears and anxieties with them as a group or with individuals in the group? Why or why not?

    d. Do you encourage others in the group to participate in the decision-making process, especially in the areas of their expertise?

3. Develop a sense of community or team spirit.

    a. Monitor your speech when you are around your people for one week. If this is too difficult for you, ask someone else such as your spouse or secretary to do it for you. When you are with your group, what pronouns do you use? Are they *I* and *my* or *we* and *our*?

b. How much time do you spend together with your group? Is it mostly for business or for pleasure or both? Do you ever have fun together away from the office?

c. How much time do you spend with the individuals who make up the group? Does it include pleasure as well as business? Have you ever invited any of them into your home for some fellowship and fun? Do you find yourself avoiding anyone in particular? Who is it? Why? Are your reasons valid?

4. Keep the lines of communication open.

a. How well does your team communicate?

b. Are you aware of any unresolved conflicts between people in your group including yourself?

c. When there is a conflict, do the people in your group go to one another privately to seek resolution? Why or why not?

This worksheet is not intended to be a once-and-for-all tool but should help you with implementing your dream. I suggest that you use it on an annual basis.

7

OVERCOMING OBSTINATE OBSTACLES

Implementing Your Vision, Part 2

It would be a mistake for a pastor to assume that because a number of people are committed to the church's vision, it is certain to be implemented. The problem is that certain obstacles are sure to surface that have the potential to discourage the team or divert its attention from the dream. This is destined to take place in any ministry organization, whether it is a church or a parachurch. There may be several obstacles that affect the church. One is people who are committed to preserving the church's status quo. Their mantra is "Come weal or come woe our status is quo." Another obstacle is those who object to the ministry's music, some preferring traditional and some contemporary. A third is people who worry that bringing unchurched adults and their kids to church will affect its direction adversely. And a fourth obstacle is those who are convinced that every service should end with a gospel presentation followed by an altar call.

In the previous chapter I said that team building is necessary to accomplish two agendas. First, it is necessary to craft a team of people who are in a position to influence the vision. This is usually accomplished when the visionary leader understands the importance of the team (step 1), recruits the team (step 2), and crafts the team (step 3). The latter is accomplished by an understanding of commitment and cooperation and the need for catalyzing that commitment.

The second agenda is to craft a ministry team in such a way that people keep moving in the right direction despite various obstinate obstacles, such as the four mentioned above, that impede their progress. This is accomplished in the fourth and fifth steps of the team building process covered in this chapter: empowering the team and encouraging the team.

Empowering the Team

The fourth step in building the team is to empower the team. Empowerment is an important concept in leadership. In defining the term for businesses, Jay Conger writes, "Empowerment, then, is essentially a process of strengthening subordinates' convictions in their own self-efficacy."[1] I would redefine the term in the Christian context: empowerment is the process of strengthening the team members' beliefs in their ability to overcome potential vision-blocking obstacles through their resources in Christ. Conger's definition rests solely on various God-given talents and abilities that reside to a certain extent within all people. In general, these are present at birth and may be developed through training. My definition includes Conger's natural gifts and abilities, which are, indeed, from God, but I add the supernatural dimension that every believer has through Christ. These concepts will be explored later.

Conger further explains the importance of empowerment when he writes, "These beliefs are critical because they determine the extent to which people will initiate and persist in attempts to master difficult experiences."[2] The principle is rather simple. If people do not believe they can overcome certain obstacles on the way to accomplishing their goals, they will fail. This is true regardless of the nature of the obstacles or their personal ability to cope with them. This explains why some very obviously gifted people fail miserably in life, while those who appear less talented are successful. Whereas some people will avoid situations they mistakenly believe are beyond their abilities, others will attempt the impossible.

The obvious lesson for visionary leadership is that successful leaders help their people realize their tremendous potential to overcome seemingly impossible tasks. Conger further elaborates:

> In essence, then, empowerment heightens a person's willingness to attempt difficult tasks and to make sustained efforts without necessarily a concern for positive outcomes. Tasks that would have been judged too difficult are now perceived as feasible. Empowerment is critical for charismatic leaders because it allows them to mobilize their organization in the face of monumental challenges. Even though high and sometimes unrealistic expectations may be set by the leader, they will be accepted.[3]

Thus, through empowerment, team members will take a more positive approach toward overcoming vision obstacles whether they think they will succeed or not. But how does a visionary leader empower his team to approach obstacles in this manner? There are at least six ways to accomplish this.

Empowerment through Self-Worth

Visionary leaders empower their teams by helping them recognize their true value and significance in light of the grace of God through Jesus Christ. Many Christians, including seasoned leaders and board members, face a constant struggle with their feelings of self-worth. The problem is that we live in a real world filled with pain, rejection, and failure. The problem-free life is a fiction. Life is a series of experiences that make constant assaults on our self-worth. Therefore, when various obstinate obstacles or difficulties challenge, people may or may not respond well depending on their present emotional state. If they are experiencing low self-esteem, they may give up without firing a shot. If they are feeling good about their worth, they may tackle the problem head-on and win.

The answer to this problem is for visionary leaders first to understand for themselves and then to teach their people the doctrine of God's grace and how it affects the Christian's daily life. In Romans 5:2 Paul states that through Jesus Christ "we have obtained our introduction by faith into this grace in which we stand." Not only are we saved by grace through faith (Eph. 2:8–9), but we are also to live by grace each day of our lives. Grace does not take a vacation after the cross. That sounds good, but what does that mean? Even more important, what does it have to do with a Christian's self-esteem?

In his book *The Search for Significance*, Robert McGee writes:

> Whether labeled "self-esteem" or "self-worth," the feeling of significance is crucial to man's emotional, spiritual, and social stability, and is the driving element within the human spirit. Understanding this single need opens the door to understanding our actions and attitudes.[4]

He further points out that our hunger for self-worth is God given and only can be satisfied through a relationship with him. In fact, God in his love for us through the grace of Christ has already met all of our esteem needs.

McGee is a professional Christian counselor and the founder and president of Rapha, a nationally recognized health care organization that provides in-hospital and out-patient care with a Christ-centered perspective for adults and adolescents suffering psychiatric and substance abuse problems. He indicates that through his study of the Scriptures and his counseling interaction with people, he has discovered four obstacles that plague the majority of people in their search for significance.

PERFORMANCE

The first obstacle to a sense of significance is the belief that we must perform and meet certain standards to feel good about ourselves. The symptoms of this belief are such things as the fear of failure, perfectionism, manipulation, an intense drive or desire for success, and an avoidance of risks. We must realize that our value does not depend on our abilities to meet certain standards, whether our own or others, but on what Jesus Christ accomplished at the cross, in particular justification. According to Romans 5:1, we have been justified in God's eyes through faith in Christ. This means that we already have his righteousness or perfection not through what we do but through what he has done for us at the cross. The standard has already been met, and we are now fully pleasing to our Father. In effect, to attempt to meet certain standards for our self-worth is fruitless, because the standard has already been met through our justification. We do not need to strive after what we already have. As they say in Texas, "It's a done deal."[5]

ACCEPTANCE

The second obstacle to a sense of significance is the belief that we must be accepted by others to feel significant. Some of the symptoms of this belief are such things as the fear of rejection, the desire to please others regardless of the cost, an unusual sensitivity to criticism, and withdrawal to avoid criticism. But God, because of his grace in Jesus Christ, has met this problem as well, in particular through reconciliation. According to Colossians 1:21–22, we have been reconciled to God through the cross of Christ. In Christ we have God's complete and unconditional acceptance. As a result, our acceptance and worth are not dependent on other people because we are fully pleasing and totally accepted in Christ.[6]

BLAME

The third obstacle to a sense of significance is the belief that when we fail, we are unworthy of love and deserve to be punished. The symptoms of this belief are self-blame, blaming others rather than ourselves when we fail, the fear of punishment, punishing others, and the drive to avoid failure at all costs. The solution is the grace of God in Christ, in particular propitiation. According to 1 John 4:9–11, Jesus Christ became the propitiation or satisfaction for our sins. He satisfied the wrath of God by taking our punishment on himself. Therefore we no longer have to fear punishment or shift our blame to others because Christ paid for all of our sins at the cross.[7]

SHAME

The fourth obstacle to a sense of significance is the belief that we are what we are; we cannot change. Therefore we are hopeless. The symptoms are feelings of shame, hopelessness, and inferiority. There also may be isolation and withdrawal from others. Again, the solution is God's grace in Christ, in particular regeneration. According to John 3:3–6 and other passages, we have become a new creation in Christ. We have changed because he has imparted new life to us through the cross of Christ. Regeneration is not our work but the work of the Holy Spirit, who makes each one of us a new person the very moment we trust Christ. We no longer need to feel hopeless, shameful, or inferior because in Christ we are no longer the people we were without Christ.[8]

Ultimately what we learn from God's loving grace through Jesus Christ is that not only did God provide sufficient grace to save us but that grace also continues to operate and liberate us from the various obstacles that seek to demean us and lower our personal worth in our own eyes. Jesus Christ is our single source of security and the only basis for our self-worth.

To understand this divine truth and begin to live accordingly—to grasp our real worth and significance in Christ—allows visionary leaders to approach the various obstacles that come into their lives and ministries with a totally different attitude. In whatever they do, it would be nice to have the approval and acceptance of their peers and friends, but when (not if) they do not receive that acceptance and approval, leaders are still unconditionally loved, accepted, and valued by God through Christ. This knowledge is refreshing and liberating and allows Christians to approach leadership with a totally different perspective. They are no longer afraid to tackle ministry-related or personal problems head-on, and they take good risks because their self-worth is not dependent on their success or acceptance by others but on God's unconditional grace in Jesus Christ.

It is imperative that visionary leaders incorporate this truth into their lives and then, in turn, teach this truth verbally and by example to those who make up their teams. Once leaders have implemented this grace in their lives, they must treat people accordingly. In what they say and do, they must value others as persons just as Christ values them. Next, leaders teach the truths of God's grace. In fact, teaching these truths alone has the potential to empower a leadership team to accomplish their dream. But there is more.

Obstacles	Solution
Performance	Justification—Romans 5:1
Acceptance	Reconciliation—Colossians 1:21–22
Blame	Propitiation—1 John 4:9–11
Shame	Regeneration—John 3:3–6

Empowerment through Personal Confidence

Visionary leaders empower their teams by developing each person's confidence in his or her abilities to be used by God. Not only do Christians struggle with feelings of insignificance, but they also tend to demean their individual abilities to handle tasks and obstacles for God. They lack self-confidence. They view themselves as either average or below par in their capacity to be used of God. When they encounter obstacles, they often react with low expectations of themselves and little assurance of ministry accomplishment.

While this may not be a constant in their lives, it has a way of cropping up periodically and hindering their pursuit of sustained excellence in their ministries for Christ. Thus it is imperative that leaders train and encourage their organizational teams to approach their leadership and ministries with a bold confidence in their God-given abilities. There are several reasons Christians can be confident.

DIVINE DESIGN

Each Christian has been divinely designed and enabled by God for service. To denigrate our abilities is to denigrate his special design and work in our lives. At birth God uniquely blessed each of us with certain natural talents, abilities, and temperaments to be used for him. At the point of conversion, he added certain God-given spiritual gifts. This affects such areas of our lives as our work and how we learn.

As long as we operate within this design, we must realize that we can overcome huge obstacles and accomplish great things for God. Rather than denigrate our abilities, we should regularly celebrate them as God's design. In light of this, every ministry for Christ, whether church or parachurch, should develop a program of assessment to help its people discover and then properly implement their divine design. This will enable them to come much closer to realizing their full potential for Christ and his ministry.[9]

MINISTRY NICHE

Since God has uniquely designed and gifted all believers, each has a ministry niche where he or she can excel. The idea here is that every believer is a "ten" somewhere.[10] This truth should encourage all believers and inspire them to discover their design and to become actively involved in their particular ministry area. This enables them to experience all the excitement and benefits that result from ministering with sustained excellence.

156

DIVINE EMPOWERMENT

We can be confident in our abilities because God indwells each of us at the point of conversion and empowers those natural abilities to be used for him. Paul asks in 1 Corinthians 6:19, "Or do you not know that your body is a temple of the Holy Spirit who is in you, whom you have from God, and that you are not your own?" This passage teaches an amazing truth of Christianity: God in some way takes up residence in our lives. One result of his indwelling is our empowerment to act in life. Thus in Colossians 1:29 Paul could write, "For this purpose also I labor, striving according to His power, which mightily works within me."

God's power makes it possible for us to accomplish far more than most people understand. I believe that a large number of Christians fail to realize their full potential in Christ because they are not aware of all that he can accomplish through them as the result of his indwelling and empowering them. As I noted earlier, an example is the church at Ephesus. To this church Paul wrote, "Now to Him who is able to do far more abundantly beyond all that we ask or think, according to the power that works within us" (Eph. 3:20). He warned those believers that they were not thinking and asking big enough, in light of the power of the indwelling Holy Spirit. As a result, they were missing the realization of their full potential for God.

> **THREE REASONS PEOPLE SHOULD BE CONFIDENT**
> 1. God has uniquely designed and gifted them.
> 2. All have a ministry niche where they excel.
> 3. The Spirit indwells and empowers them for their ministry.

Empowerment through Servant-Leadership

Visionary leaders empower their teams by personally serving their teams. The model for leadership found in the New Testament is that of servant-leadership. Jesus Christ established this model when he led and served his disciples during his ministry on earth. In a discussion of the difference between his leadership and pagan leadership, the Savior says in Matthew 20:26–28, "It is not this way among you, but whoever wishes to become great among you shall be your servant, and whoever wishes to be first among you shall be your slave; just as the Son of Man did not come to be served, but to serve, and to give His life a ransom for many."

It is most important to note that while Christ was on earth, he did not spend all of his time with the multitudes but spent much of his time pouring his life into his disciples. Robert Coleman writes, "He actually spent more time with His disciples than with everybody else in the world put together. He ate with them, slept with them, and talked with them for the most part of His entire active ministry."[11] Coleman further observes, "Contrary to what one might expect, as the ministry of Christ lengthened into the second and third years, He gave increasingly more time to the chosen disciples, not less."[12]

In light of the impact the disciples had on the world, we understand why Jesus spent so much time with them. Who would have ever imagined that such a small band of socially and politically insignificant people could turn the world upside down (Acts 17:6)? However, as I study various models of leadership in the church in particular, I find that we have failed to catch the significance of what the Savior did. Very few pastors spend enough time with their leadership teams to exercise servant-leadership.

I believe that a primary reason for this is today's prevailing cultural model for pastoral ministry. Although we are slow to acknowledge it, our culture plays a bigger role in what pastors do in ministry than we realize. I strongly contend that the cultural model for many of today's pastors, especially in small churches, is based on a rural model where the average pastor spends much of his time visiting his people, along with officiating at weddings and funerals, and preparing some sermons. That is what they expect, and that is usually what they get. The people who make up the boards primarily serve not by shepherding the flock (Acts 20:28; 1 Pet. 5:1–2) but by meeting once a month to make decisions regarding what is often mundane. Therefore little time is left over for pastors to exercise servant-leadership, developing leaders who, in turn, shepherd the flock.

Our times and the culture have changed since our churches adopted this rural model. The population has shifted from rural to urban America. But people's expectations of what pastors do somehow did not make the transition. The larger urban and suburban churches have forced some change because the senior pastor cannot be expected to visit everyone in the church. Thus administrative responsibilities have replaced visitation responsibilities in many job descriptions, although some larger churches have hired a minister of visitation. In either case pastors are not spending much time with their staff or board members.

This is the reason I proposed in chapter 3 a new model for pastoral ministry. It is one that I believe includes more of the biblical essentials for ministry. In that model I placed the development of a team of leaders as a top priority for pastors in the church. This is a crucial aspect of servant-leadership that no longer can be neglected if our churches are going to reach the growing number of nonchurched Americans.

Just as important, when pastors or parachurch leaders serve and pour time into their teams, it sends a clear message that these people are important and valued by the ministry. Once leaders have gained credibility with their teams, the fact that they take time out of their busy schedules to be with their people, to minister to their spiritual and emotional needs and to train them for leadership in the church, has a way of motivating them for ministry. They, in turn, will repeat the process with others all the way down to the lowliest member. It would be comparable to someone with the stature of a man like Billy Graham taking time to minister to you or me. We would feel honored and challenged to accomplish great things for our Savior as a response to that kind of servant's heart.

159

Empowerment through Accomplishment

Visionary leaders empower their teams through individual and institutional accomplishment. Team members experience success individually in their separate ministry tasks, and the organization as a whole experiences success in its ministry. As a result, all of those who are a part of the organization feel a sense of accomplishment.

INDIVIDUAL ACCOMPLISHMENT

It is important that team members experience individual accomplishments in a ministry. When this happens, they realize what God can do through them and are motivated to attempt even greater things for God. Wise visionary leaders will seek to involve their people in tasks commensurate with their abilities according to their divine design.

Most good dreams are large and all-encompassing and span a significant period of time. While initially this serves to challenge the ministry community, over the long haul big visions can appear unattainable. This may overwhelm and bring discouragement in spite of a person's knowledge of his or her divine design. The solution to this potential problem is for leaders to put on their management hats and exercise their skills in planning. Though more will be said about this area of management in the next chapter, wise planning instructs us to break the dream into accomplishable, "bite-size" tasks.

In *The Leadership Challenge* Kouzes and Posner suggest that the term *planning* fails to convey the emotions that are experienced when someone accomplishes a significant task. They have come up with the more descriptive term *small wins*.[13] Bite-size tasks result in small wins, which encourage people and build their commitment to a dream. In light of this, leaders should plan the team's various ministries and break them down in such a way that team members are able to accomplish them with success. Furthermore, as Kouzes and Posner write:

Small wins build people's confidence levels and reinforce their natural desire to feel successful. Since additional resources generally tend to flow to winners, this means that slightly larger wins can be attempted next. A series of small wins therefore provides a foundation of stable building blocks. Each win preserves gains and makes it harder to return to pre-existing conditions. Like miniature experiments or pilot studies, small wins also provide information that facilitates learning and adaptation."[14]

Nehemiah practiced the strategy of taking bite-size tasks and accomplishing small wins. This is clearly portrayed in Nehemiah 3, where the work of rebuilding the wall and gates is assigned to various people on the team. It appears that certain individuals were assigned various sections of the wall or gates for repair. One group repaired one of the gates (v. 13), while another group made repairs along the wall (v. 15).

I once implemented a small-wins policy at a church that was in desperate need of renewal. This church, like so many today across America, had been declining in attendance for several years, and some members were even questioning whether they should continue. I was asked to serve as an interim pastor until they located a new person. As I suspected, the church had no ministry vision. Consequently, I began to cast a Great Commission dream for reaching the nonchurched people in the church's community. While the people were excited about the prospect of reaching the nonchurched, how could they accomplish such a task when they were so few in number? The obvious answer was to implement a process of small wins.

To begin, we invited the nonchurched people in the community to hear a seeker-friendly sermon from the Scriptures. A seeker-friendly sermon addresses some relevant topic such as discouragement, fear, or anger in such a way that both churched and nonchurched people benefit from the message.

A problem was that over the years, as attendance declined, so had the church's enthusiasm for maintaining the facility where they met. The people had become used to the situation and were blind to the deterioration of the buildings. As a new person at the church, I noticed it immediately and realized that visitors would also. Facilities in need of repair communicate a loser's image to the community. Naturally people question the credibility of any group that would allow such conditions to continue.

We set up a small win: repairing and painting the facilities. I preached a positive sermon that explained how cutting-edge churches work hard to maintain the appearance of their facilities. Since this church had caught the vision, they immediately organized a series of workdays to repair and improve the facility so that, at the very least, it would appear presentable. Quickly the members realized that this goal was bite-size and easily attainable. Once they had accomplished this task, they felt good about their work and, even more important, about themselves. The next bite-size task would be even more attainable in light of their accomplishment.

The important lesson here is that not only was the facility improved but so was the congregation's personal esteem. People who had viewed themselves as losers now, through their accomplishment, began to see themselves as winners. This is inevitable when a ministry community experiences a series of wins; how could they view themselves in any other way?

Of course there will be failures. Many young leaders, whether professional or lay, will not take risks because they fear failure. They believe that if they fail, then those on the leadership team will lose confidence in their ability to lead. For this reason it is important to develop an environment where it is permissible to fail. A leader must be willing to fail to succeed. If an environment has not been established where people have the freedom to fail, then they will not take risks, and the ministry will either plateau or go into decline.

INSTITUTIONAL ACCOMPLISHMENT

Not only do visionary leaders empower their teams through encouraging individual accomplishment, they may do so directly or indirectly through institutional accomplishment as well. In this context I use *institutional accomplishment* in two ways.

The first is the general success of the church or parachurch ministry as a whole. Successful ministries in themselves empower those on the ministry team. It is hard to argue against success. Small bites and small wins eventually encourage and lead to large bites and large wins. Tired ministry organizations renew themselves and begin to grow again. New ministries start to grow and become larger established churches or parachurch organizations. Ministry tasks that were viewed as much too difficult are now seen as accomplishable. Visionary leaders must be sure to continue the small-wins strategy while pointing to God's obvious blessing of the team's efforts.

Institutional accomplishment is also God's hand of blessing on a ministry. People are empowered when they sense that God is uniquely blessing and honoring their ministry in a way that is not common in other ministries. There is a special sense that God is in this work. Therefore visionary leaders should be unusually sensitive to these signs and take opportunity to point them out to their ministry teams. In addition, they can regularly remind them of God's blessings and use them when they recast the dream to "rally the troops," especially during any lulls in the ministry.

Nehemiah provides us with an example of this kind of empowerment. In Nehemiah 2:17–18 he conveys his dream to the Jews who had survived the captivity and were living in reproach in Jerusalem. Immediately prior to his charge to accomplish the dream, he calls their attention to the fact that God has uniquely blessed his efforts thus far (v. 18). He refers to such inspiring events as God using the pagan King Artaxerxes to allow him to return to Jerusalem and issue letters that would give him access to material with which they could rebuild the gates and wall (v. 8). This provides the hope and encouragement they had been waiting for. In spite of their desperate situation, there is little question that God is behind Nehemiah's vision and will bless their efforts to rebuild the wall.

This knowledge of God's special blessing has so affected and empowered Nehemiah that he also refers to it when he faces Israel's enemies. For example, in Nehemiah 2:19 Sanballat and Tobiah mock the Jews and their vision. However, Nehemiah, in the context of his vision message, calls attention to the fact that God will give them success (v. 20). Most likely this is based on God's unique work in the past. I suspect it may have been said within hearing distance of the Jews, although there is no evidence for this in the text.

Empowerment through Delegation

Visionary leaders empower their ministry teams through granting them the opportunity and authority to lead in their areas of ministry influence. There is some debate in leadership circles concerning where the authority to exercise that power rests in an organization. While this is not as much an issue in parachurch ministries, it is in some churches. I refer primarily to churches that are congregational in nature or that exercise elder rule. Without going into great detail, I will say there may be a power struggle between the pastor and the board over who leads and the amount of power and authority behind that leadership. Some churches have adopted a form of lay co-leadership that puts the power in the hands of a lay-elder board. In this scheme, often the pastor's leadership role is that he functions as "just another one of the boys." The problem here is that co-leadership results in no leadership. Based on Scripture and experience, I believe the authority scales tip in the favor of the senior pastor, who has been trained for leadership as well as preaching and teaching. He must remember, though, that he is to lead not as a tyrant (Matt. 20:25) but as a servant (Mark 10:45).

Assuming that the power to lead and the authority to exercise that power are resident in the ministry organization's primary leader, he in turn will empower his team members by granting them the authority necessary to work within their ministry spheres of influence. Again, there has always been a problem in organizations where the person who has power is afraid to delegate that power, rendering those under him practically powerless to accomplish their tasks. In Christian ministry this must not be the case because God has designed and granted gifts to each believer in the body of Christ for ministry (Romans 12; 1 Corinthians 12; Ephesians 4).

Visionary leaders empower their team members to make the key decisions affecting their particular ministry areas. This means they are free to make key decisions without checking with the primary leader. This also assumes that the leader is training and coaching them so they have the expertise to make these kinds of decisions. This is esteem building and communicates confidence in the ministry team.

There are several biblical examples of this kind of delegation. In Nehemiah 7:1–3 it appears that Nehemiah delegated his leadership power and authority in this manner. In verse 2 he places Hanani, his brother, and Hananiah, his military commander, in charge of Jerusalem. Along with this delegation, he gives them some coaching (v. 3). In Exodus 18 Jethro, Moses's father-in-law, observes how much of Moses's time is spent in settling the disputes of the people of Israel. Then he provides Moses with some excellent advice, for he points out the need to delegate much of this responsibility to other competent, qualified people (vv. 17–23). Moses gives these men the power and authority to settle all minor disputes while he handles the major disputes (v. 26).

Empowerment through Modeling

Visionary leaders empower their teams through their own examples of sustained excellence. Leaders themselves are examples of what the ministry organization is all about. To understand a

165

ministry and its mission, observe the leader, which is exactly what people on the ministry team do.

This comes as no surprise to those in Christian leadership, because repeatedly Scripture emphasizes the importance of personal example for others. On numerous occasions Paul exhorts his followers not only to observe his example but also to follow his example: 1 Corinthians 4:14–17; 11:1; Philippians 3:17; 4:9; and 1 Thessalonians 1:6. In 2 Thessalonians 3:8–9, Paul states that he paid for his own food and worked to meet his own support needs to be a model and an example to the believers in the church at Thessalonica. Whether their lives are good or bad, leaders are models to their followers. Paul's desire was to provide a model of sustained excellence that would attract disciples and bring glory to his Savior. Modeling empowers a team in several important ways.

CREDIBILITY AND EMULATION

Leaders whose lives are consistent with what they profess both gain credibility and encourage their followers to emulate their behavior. Although leaders have the authority to exercise power, it is their behavior not their position that brings them respect and credibility. Paul acknowledges this truth in 1 Corinthians 9:1–19, where he alludes to his rights as an apostle but states that he has chosen not to exercise these rights because of some potential negative impact on his leadership and the preaching of the gospel (vv. 15–19).

That same behavior not only gains leaders credibility but also gives incentive for others to behave in a similar way and become models in their own right. Paul describes this in 1 Thessalonians 1:5–7:

> For our gospel did not come to you in word only, but also in power and in the Holy Spirit and with full conviction; just as you know what kind of men we proved to be among you for your sake. You also became imitators of us and of the Lord, having received the word in

much tribulation with the joy of the Holy Spirit, so that you became an example to all the believers in Macedonia and in Achaia.

VALUES

Personal examples empower followers by imparting to them what leaders value, the things most important to them, which penetrate to the very depth of their being and give meaning to their lives. Values affect every area of life and belief and exert a profound influence on co-workers. Kouzes and Posner cite research that shows effective companies communicate their values through clarity, consensus, and intensity.[15]

Good visionary leaders incarnate their values clearly by preaching and living them to such an extent that those who make up the ministry team are able to articulate them. Good visionary leaders live and communicate their values in such a way that their teams know what they are and are committed to them. This is ministry consensus. It is prevalent in parachurch ministries because their values are extremely focused and pronounced. They are known in the Christian community for those particular values, and the ministry team is recruited because of an affinity for them. Supporters select and contribute to these ministries because of a commitment to these same values. The typical American evangelical church has a strong set of values. The ministry team is recruited on the basis of their commitment to these values, and most on the ministry team, if you should ask, would consider dying for them.

Good visionary leaders feel very strongly about certain values. They are held with intensity. It is not that they merely agree with certain values but that those values are esteemed and practiced almost daily. People do not have to be reminded periodically of these values, for they are ingrained in everything the leader does. As I have said, this is the heart of the parachurch movement. Most parachurch organizations hold certain biblical values with intensity. Most likely, the founder of the organization was deeply affected by those values, and his or her life has mirrored them consistently in their public and private ministries. If a parachurch ministry begins to plateau or decline, it is often because the founder dies and is replaced by someone who holds the same values with less intensity, or because the organization has not developed more culturally relevant ways of implementing those values in the ministry.

I believe that one of the reasons nine out of ten churches in America are either stagnant or dying is the lack of intensity in holding their values, whatever they may be. I suspect that all of those that are evangelical, and there are many in that 90 percent, have strong doctrinal statements. If you were to ask them what they believe, they could quickly and vigorously produce a doctrinal statement. And the members of those churches agree with that doctrinal statement. While they have clarity and consensus on their values, they come up short on intensity. If on a Sunday morning you were to step into the pulpit and ask how many people believe evangelism is important, all would raise their hands. That reflects clarity and consensus. However, if you were to ask how many people had presented the gospel of Christ to some other person within the last few months, very few hands would go up. That reflects a lack of intensity.

Those evangelical churches that are growing as a result of conversion growth usually are led by people who value the Great Commission with intensity. They do not simply talk about evangelism and edification—they vigorously evangelize people using culturally relevant and effective methods. Evangelism and edification are major topics of discussion and are highly esteemed among those on the ministry team. When they tell stories, they usually are about how someone came to faith or is growing in and proclaiming the faith (edification). Even among the members are intense feelings about seeing people come to faith who are followed up through a program of aggressive

> ### SIX WAYS TO EMPOWER A TEAM
> 1. Self-worth
> 2. Personal confidence
> 3. Servant-leadership
> 4. Accomplishment
> 5. Delegation
> 6. Modeling

edification. But the important thing to remember in all this is that their feelings reflect those of the pastor of the church. They look to him as the mission point person to model how they should behave.

Encouraging the Team

The fifth step in building the team is to encourage the team. I suspect that there is some overlap between empowering a team and encouraging a team. Together the two help a team overcome the various obstacles (such as those found at the beginning of this chapter) they are sure to meet as they move toward the vision.

The concepts of empowering the team and encouraging the team approach handling obstacles from two angles. On the one hand, empowerment prepares the team and each of its members to encounter and overcome various obstacles. On the other hand, encouragement helps the team and any of its people who have been snagged and held up by an obstacle to break free. Encouragement jump-starts a ministry whose battery is run-down or provides a sudden burst of energy to help it through a difficult time. No matter how empowered a group may be, if it faces enough obstacles, the ministry will slow down. Encouragement reaches out a helping hand to those on the team who are discouraged and have already dropped out or are contemplating doing so (Acts 14:21–22).

The Problem of Discouragement

I have discovered over the years as a church pastor and as one in a seminary who prepares men and women for ministry that discouragement is a major obstacle (if not *the* major obstacle) to ministry and the accomplishment of a dream. Just recently I read a letter from a young man in pastoral ministry in the Midwest. The letter was addressed to his friends letting them know that he was dropping out of the ministry for a while to recuperate from the discouragement and depression he had experienced as the result of attempting to plant a church and failing. He had decided to start a church but did not have adequate preparation. As he and his small team attempted to move forward, they encountered waves of obstacles that took a heavy toll. Discouragement set in, quickly followed by depression, which led to the pastor's eventual resignation from the team. As I read the letter, I caught in his words such an overwhelming sense of failure that I question if he will ever return to professional pastoral ministry.

We must keep in mind that discouragement can happen to the best of us. No one is exempt. For example, one of the most discouraging portions of Scripture is 2 Timothy 4:9–16. The entire section, which was written toward the end of Paul's life, drips with discouragement. Why was he so discouraged? First, many of his friends had deserted him at a time when he needed their support (vv. 10, 16). Second, his enemies, in particular Alexander the coppersmith, had attacked him (vv. 14–15). Finally, except for Luke's company, he was all alone in a Roman dungeon (v. 11). Perhaps he sensed that the end was near (v. 6), because, according to tradition, he was beheaded soon after he wrote these words. Discouragement attacks anyone regardless of race, creed, or religion. It is no respecter of persons. It does not care if you are one of Christ's apostles, the leader of a team, or a team member.

The Solution of Encouragement

The obvious solution to the obstacle of discouragement is encouragement. Visionary leaders must spend time encouraging their ministry teams. It provides team members with hope that helps them break free from the web of obstacles that hinder or momentarily slow them down.

I believe that one of the keys to the success of Paul's early ministry was his teammate Barnabas. God's distinctive mark on Barnabas's life was his ability to encourage. In fact, though his name was Joseph, according to Acts 4:36, he was called Barnabas by the apostles, which means "son of encouragement." We get a glimpse of why in Acts 11:22–23 when the church at Jerusalem sent him to Antioch, where he encouraged the believers to remain true to the Lord.

But how might a leader encourage people on a regular basis? What can he do to assign encouragement its proper place in his team-crafting efforts? It's interesting that not much has been written in leadership material on encouragement. However, Kouzes and Posner have recognized the importance of encouragement to leadership and in *The Leadership Challenge* have assigned it a major section (two chapters) titled "Encouraging the Heart." They suggest that leaders encourage their people in two ways: by recognizing individual achievements and by celebrating the efforts of the entire group.[16] Both methods are reflected in the Scriptures.

Recognize Individual Achievements

Visionary leaders encourage their teams by recognizing their people and their individual ministry accomplishments. This is because God values people and what they do for his glory. In spite of the fall, people are still valuable and important to God. He created them in his image (Gen. 1:26–27). In Matthew 6:26 the Savior indicates that human life is worth far more than animal life. Then in Mark 8:36–37 Jesus asserts that a man's soul is far more valuable than the wealth and possessions of the entire world. God also values people's work when it is done for him (Eph. 6:5–8; Col. 3:22–25).

Visionary leaders should expect the best from themselves and their team members. Kouzes and Posner state that "successful leaders have high expectations, both of themselves and of their followers."[17] I find that often this is not the case in many ministry organizations, especially the church. Far too many settle for mediocrity in ministry. Perhaps this is because so many churches are small and viewed as extended families; consequently, the family does not mind as much if a member who is a Sunday school teacher is winging it. The important thing is that the kids have a teacher, and the fact that the individual cannot teach is something to deal with later. While members do not notice it, today's nonchurched visitors who are used to excellence do notice it.

Scripture encourages the pursuit of excellence. Excellence was important in the Old Testament. Worship was characterized by excellence. The Jews were to offer only their best animals as sacrifices to God in their worship (Lev. 22:20, 22). Excellence was important as well in the New Testament. A man's work was to be accomplished "as to the Lord, and not to men" (Eph. 6:7; see also Col. 3:23). Excellence also characterizes God and what he does. He gave his very best when he gave us his Son, Jesus Christ.

God values people's best accomplishments for him and rewards these works. Scripture has much to say about rewards (1 Cor. 3:8, 10–15; 4:5; 9:17). In the future, at the judgment seat of Christ (2 Cor. 5:10), God will reward the Christian's works (1 Cor. 3:10–15). It is important to note that the basis for this reward is said to be "the quality of each man's work" (v. 13). If God values people and their good works of service for him, then it makes sense that we do the same. As a pastor in one church, I did not believe in publicly acknowledging people for God's accomplishments through their lives. My reasoning was that I was afraid I might leave someone out and offend him or her. Of course this is always a danger, but the opposite extreme of not giving due recognition, in my opinion, is far worse.

Leaders, then, must seek to avoid two extremes. One extreme is when they err by failing to recognize any of the accomplishments of their people. This sends a clear message that who they are and what they do is not important. The result is that people stop caring and the ministry begins to die. The other extreme is when they err by attempting to recognize everything a person does. The problem here is that after a while the recognition loses its value. Leaders should seek to acknowledge the legitimate accomplishments of their people in some beneficial way that moves the ministry toward the fulfillment of its dream.

Both the church and parachurch organizations can recognize people in two ways. First, they can set up a formal system of awards. This includes such things as bonuses, raises, award ceremonies, and promotions where possible. Some ministry organizations do not practice this because they feel it is a gimmick developed by the secular world that is not necessary in God's work. This is a grave mistake because formal awards announce to those on the team that their good accomplishments for the Savior are valued. However, the problem with a formal award system is that people begin to expect them and eventually may not see them as rewards but as part of their ministry compensation.

The second way to recognize people's accomplishments is to reward them informally. This can take place either in public or in private. It includes intangible rewards such as personal recognition through verbal and written praise, thank-you notes, being personally available to them, and so on. These methods are used repeatedly in the Scriptures. For example, Paul gives public thanks for various churches in his writings and recognizes their works for the Savior (Col. 1:3–4; 1 Thess. 1:2–10). He also singles out individuals and commends them to others based on what God has done through them. He did this with Timothy (Phil. 2:19, 22), Epaphroditus (vv. 29–30), and Judas and Silas (Acts 15:25–27). I do not believe this was mere flattery or an attempt on his part to win a hearing, because on other occasions he would not praise but would confront problem churches, such as in Galatia (Gal. 1:1–10), and people who were in error, such as Peter (2:11–14).

CELEBRATE TEAM ACCOMPLISHMENTS

Not only can leaders encourage their team members individually, but they also can encourage the team as a whole. Kouzes and Posner suggest that one way to do this well is through both cheerleading and public celebration.[18]

In a very important sense, the primary leaders of ministries should be cheerleaders. Every ministry needs its cheerleaders to encourage people to work together during the tough times as well as the good times. What happens in a football game when the home team is on defense and the opposition has the ball on their one-yard line? The cheerleaders go to work, and we hear, "Push 'em back, push 'em back, way back!" The world of athletics has discovered the strength of team loyalty, why not the parachurch and the church?

It is also interesting to note that in athletics, victories are usually followed by celebrations. Athletes and fans are quick to celebrate their accomplishments. Why are many Christian organizations reluctant to do the same? They did so in the Old Testament. For example, Nehemiah led the Jews in Jerusalem in rebuilding the wall and gates of the city. This accomplished their vision. Then there was a dedication of the wall with a public celebration of worship to God, acknowledging what he had done through the people (Neh. 12:27–47). This was a time of great celebrative worship involving two choirs, a band, singing, and the offering of sacrifices.

But what do visionary leaders celebrate? By its nature, a celebration has an object; something is being recognized. Thus it makes sense to celebrate the things that are important to the ministry organization. Certainly the accomplishment of a vision is a major cause for celebration, as mirrored by the events of Nehemiah 12. Also, the accomplishment of various ministry goals that lead to the vision or the removal of obstacles that could hinder it are causes for celebration. Some ministry organizations celebrate important events.

> **WAYS TO ENCOURAGE PEOPLE**
>
> - Recognize their individual ministry accomplishments.
> - Celebrate their joint accomplishments as a team.

For example, schools have graduations and founders' day banquets. Churches celebrate the purchase or completion of new facilities, the accomplishment of a critical growth goal, or the addition of new staff. Some create special events for the purpose of celebration, such as a Celebration of Friendship Sunday. These celebrations also provide good opportunities for enhancing team relationships, the communication of ideas, good fellowship, and stress relief.

Worksheet

This worksheet is for the visionary leader who has developed a vision and is in the process of building a team to accomplish that vision. It seeks to help you handle obstinate obstacles that will affect the implementation of the vision.

Empowering Your Team

1. Make a list of the obstacles that you and your team face as you attempt to implement your ministry dream. You may want to do this by yourself and then together with your team to get their perspective. Which obstacles will prove difficult for your team to overcome?

2. As soon as possible, teach your team the critical principles of the grace of God in Jesus Christ. In analyzing yourself and those on the team, do you sense that any are struggling with their self-esteem regarding their performance, acceptance, blame, shame, or a combination of these?

3. Do you have a program to help your team and any others in your ministry discover their divine design and their ministry niche?

4. At present, would you consider yourself a servant-leader? Why or why not? Would the others on your team? Would you be willing to ask their opinion? Are you in a position in your ministry where you can pour a substantial amount of your time into the lives of your ministry team? Why or why not? What would you have to do to make this possible? Are you willing to do whatever it takes to make this a reality?

5. Review the responsibilities of those on the ministry team, including your own. Are there any areas or responsibilities you can break down into bite-size tasks?

6. Where is the power in your ministry organization, and who has the authority to exercise that power? Is it possible to delegate

power and the authority to exercise that power to those who lead in a particular ministry area?

7. Do you now model the values you affirm in your ministry? Would you be willing to say to your team, "Be imitators of me, just as I also am of Christ"?

Encouraging Your Team

1. How do you deal with personal and team discouragement in your ministry organization? What possible discouragement do you and your team now face?

2. Do you have in place both a formal and an informal award system? Are you the team cheerleader? Do you and your team ever celebrate the team's accomplishments? If so, name some of the ways in which you do this.

8

BITTERSWEET

Preserving Your Vision

There is another aspect to the implementation of a vision that few people talk about. It is the preservation of the vision. Actually this continues the implementation of the vision and is an extension of implementation. It looks at the envisioning process as a continuing process that takes place throughout the life of the ministry and seeks to facilitate that process in the face of obstacles. The focus in chapters 6 and 7 was on building a ministry team that can deal with obstacles to the accomplishment of the vision. The focus of this chapter is on helping visionary leaders, or point people in particular, to deal with specific kinds of obstacles (brought about by certain people and/or events) that are sure to surface in their personal lives and ministries as they lead their teams down the field toward the goal line.

The Problem

The problem is that obstacles can cause vision drift or vision disaster. Vision drift is a gradual, almost imperceptible moving or drifting away from the vision. Over time, the vision dissipates. You wake up one morning and the vision is gone—vanished into thin air. A solution to vision drift is the regular casting and recasting of the vision. Vision disaster is more like a train wreck. Certain people or events rise up to take on and oppose the vision head-on. These obstacles have also been known to drive good men and women from the ministry. The primary problem is that these obstacles, either separately or together, bring overwhelming discouragement into the visionary's life.

Discouragement

Visionary leaders will (not may) face opposition to their ideas and visions. Of course this news is old news to many pastors. Their response is, "Tell me something I don't already know." The problem concerns their response to that opposition. Most often the initial response is anger followed by discouragement (see Neh. 4:5; 6:9). This anger can be good because it has the potential to bring intensity to the vision. However, the discouragement can be bad because it can mean the death of the vision. I refer, for example, to the young church-planting pastor who, as I mentioned in an earlier chapter, dropped out of the ministry entirely because of his overwhelming discouragement.

HUMAN SOURCES OF DISCOURAGEMENT

There are a variety of sources of discouragement. It's not unusual for discouragement to originate with people, either outside or within the ministry organization or both. Most of Nehemiah's opposition came from Israel's unbelieving enemies, such as Sanballat, Tobiah, and Geshem (Neh. 2:19; 4:1–8). They used such devices as ridicule (2:19; 4:1–6), conspiracy (4:7–10), and rumor (vv. 11–12).

Opposition can surface among those who are a part of the organization. This happened to Nehemiah (6:10–13). Opposition from without can be beneficial, because it angers and catalyzes people to accomplish the vision. Unreasonable, misguided opposition from people within the ministry can cause the most emotional and spiritual damage to the visionary leader. I refer to these individuals as vision vampires, vision vultures, and vision firemen.

Vision Vampires

Vision vampires are people who attempt either intentionally or unintentionally to suck the lifeblood from the vision. They may be well-intentioned Christians who sincerely believe they are correct in opposing the vision and may see themselves as courageous defenders of the faith rather than defenders of the status quo, for many of them confuse the status quo with the faith.

In their thinking, liberalism has somehow crept into the organization.

This means they come out of their corner fighting and fighting hard, because they put visionary leaders in practically the same corner as theological heretics. Both must be fought with gusto if the church is to keep the faith. They seldom verbalize all this, and most would not use the term *heretic* to describe the leader, for they have no scriptural support, but their behavior betrays their attitudes.

Vision Vultures

Vision vultures are similar to the vampires but with less intensity. They attack the vision not by sucking the lifeblood from it but by attempting to pick it apart. They are vision nitpickers. They do not view visionary leaders as heretics, nor do they see themselves as crusaders who are defending the faith. They do not view change as unbiblical, nor do they call into question the dream on theological grounds. These are people who like things the way they are because they feel so intimidated and threatened by change.

In the church such people have become accustomed to sitting in pews, passing an offering plate, singing to organ music, and listening to long, loud sermons. It is not that the vision is wrong for everybody; they see it as wrong for themselves. Consequently they attack the vision not as a whole but in parts. They attempt to pick it apart one piece at a time. For a while they may complain about the sermons and how they have changed. Next they will complain about the instruments and music used in the worship service. And this may go on and on for years.

Vision Firemen

Vision firemen are leaders, or better, managers in the organization who, when they hear of a good vision, run and grab the nearest fire hose to put it out. You would hope that because they are in leadership positions they might ignite some fires, but since they are firemen they are much better at putting them out.

HUMAN SOURCES OF DISCOURAGEMENT
• Vision vampires
• Vision vultures
• Vision firemen

They are pure managers in leadership positions who do not properly understand leadership and its relationship to management. As managers, they correctly strive to produce orderly results, not change. Their favorite Bible text, though taken out of context, is 1 Corinthians 14:40: "But all things must be done properly and in an orderly manner." However, they feel threatened by innovative dreams and believe that it is in their vested interest to protect institutions from change rather than work with leaders to procure change. Since they are so often in high positions in ministry organizations, they can exert a chilling effect on dreaming and those who dare to dream.

RECOGNIZING THE SOURCES OF DISCOURAGEMENT

But how can you discover who the vision opponents are before they have had time to inflict a lot of damage? The key is to listen carefully to the water that flows from the fire hose. These vision opponents will probably reveal themselves by what they say when they have opportunity to respond to the dream. One popular, timeworn statement is, "We've never done it that way before." This is infamous among visionary church leaders and is known as the "seven last words of the church." What these vision opponents say is true. The purpose behind good visionary thinking is to be innovative and come up with new ways of doing things that are more relevant to today's fast-changing culture.

Another common problem is the fear of failure. People in general and some leaders in particular fear failure to such an extent that they will not take any risks. Some leaders believe that when they fail, they damage their credibility as leaders. While it is true that failure can damage leadership credibility, not to take good risks is to fail.[1] Most great leaders talk about how important failure is to their success. In many cases not only do they learn from their failure, but that failure also motivates success. The key is to create an environment in which it is permissible to fail.

Another popular nonvisionary quote is "It's impossible." But this is true of all big visions. In a very real sense this is how you know God is in it. He is in the business of making the impossible possible. Because I have worked with the *Myers-Briggs Type Indicator*, I realize that this response is fairly typical of those who prefer to perceive the world primarily through using the five senses, whereas those who prefer to perceive through intuition tend to be naturally more visionary.

Some other statements you may hear are: "Some people won't like it." "We can't afford it." "You're a dreamer." When you hear these, especially if they are said repeatedly, the chances are good that you are listening to a vision opponent. It is interesting that all of these statements are true. Visions always invite opposition and are not affordable, and visionaries are dreamers. Nevertheless, if we did not do things because some people would object, nothing would ever be accomplished. There is always somebody who does not like what we are doing. Many of the things we accomplish in life appear on the surface not to be affordable. And most good leaders, especially the entrepreneurial types, spend a lot of time dreaming. This was true of Albert Einstein, who on one occasion said that in his work imagination was more important than information.

In his excellent book on paradigms and the change process, *Discovering the Future*, Joel Arthur Barker lists statements that are made by those in the prevailing paradigm community (which may be loaded with vision adversaries) against paradigm shifters (visionaries):

"Why, that's impossible."

"We don't do things that way."

"It's too radical a change."

"We tried something like that before, and it didn't work."

"We would be a laughingstock."

"I wish it were that easy."

"It's against accepted policy."

"I always thought you were a little weird."

"Who told you you could change the rules?"

"Let's get back to reality."

"How dare you suggest that what we're doing is wrong?"

And the archetypal response of vision adversaries: "If you had been in this field as long as I have, you would know that what you are suggesting is absolutely absurd."[2]

OTHER SOURCES OF DISCOURAGEMENT

Sources of discouragement other than people are the four Fs: failure, fear, fatigue, and frustration. People may be involved in these as well. For example, people may frustrate us or cause us to fear. Whenever visionary leaders become discouraged, it will most likely involve one of these four or a combination of them.

Failure

Failure as a cause of discouragement is illustrated in Nehemiah 4:7–10 when Israel's enemies Sanballat, Tobiah, and others conspired to attack the Jews in Jerusalem. The news of this conspiracy took a heavy toll of discouragement on the people. One result was the potential failure of the vision, for they said, "And we ourselves are unable to rebuild the wall." It is true that we can learn from failure, and good leaders are motivated by failure, but failure can sap people's confidence as well and discourage them from attempting to realize the vision, as it did the Jews in Nehemiah's day.

Fear

While failure may teach and motivate, fear can paralyze. It has the awesome potential to make cowards of us all. To distract the Jews from their vision, Sanballat, Tobiah, and the rest conspired to attack and kill them (Neh. 4:7–11). When word of the conspiracy arrived in Jerusalem, Nehemiah was forced to act quickly to counter the fear that was building in his people.

Later Sanballat tried a different ploy, threatening to send a false message to Artaxerxes that Nehemiah was planning to set himself up as a king in Jerusalem. Artaxerxes would react quickly and brutally. Nehemiah responded quickly. He explained, "For all of them were trying to frighten us, thinking, 'They will become discouraged with the work and it will not be done'" (6:9).

Fatigue

Fatigue also discouraged the Jews under Nehemiah's leadership. According to Nehemiah 4:10 the people were beginning to lose physical strength, which contributed to their general discouragement. At times our bodies must rest if we are to serve our Savior with excellence. When fatigue sets in, we become more vulnerable to our sinful nature and discouragement in general. I suspect this is what the Savior had in mind in Matthew 26:40–45 and particularly in verse 41 when he says, "Keep watching and praying that you may not enter into temptation; the spirit is willing, but the flesh is weak." In times of discouragement, perhaps the best thing to do is go to bed and get some needed rest.

Frustration

The frustration recorded in Nehemiah 4:10–11 resulted from a combination of several factors. Although the Jews were physically fatigued and the work was coming to a stop, much work had to be done to clear away all the rubble. Add to this a frustrating environment of fear from their enemies who had threatened their lives, and the result could be the death of the vision, for they had stopped rebuilding the wall (v. 15).

> **FOUR SOURCES OF DISCOURAGEMENT**
> 1. Failure
> 2. Fear
> 3. Fatigue
> 4. Frustration

The Solution

I stated at the beginning of this chapter that an often overlooked aspect of the envisioning process is the preservation of the vision. A ministry organization can be well on its way to the realization of its vision when certain obstacles surface and overwhelm the visionary leader, which results in the untimely death of the vision. The primary obstacle is discouragement.

I believe that more leaders drop out of the ministry because of discouragement than any other problem in ministry, including immorality or the mishandling of the organization's funds. Indeed, discouragement will be one of the great tests of a visionary leader and his or her leadership. What should leaders do when they find themselves deeply discouraged and ready to quit?

The obvious solution to discouragement is encouragement. But what is encouragement all about, and how can leaders find encouragement when they face obstacle giants in their ministries?

After the death of Moses, God appointed Joshua as the new leader of his people Israel. God's mission for Joshua was to lead his people into the land, a mission fraught with many obstacles that would easily leave even the strongest leader discouraged. God anticipated this, and his message for Joshua is found in Joshua 1:6–9 when he commands him to be strong and courageous to fend off discouragement. But how is this done? The following are several truths that answer this question.

Recognize That Discouragement Is Universal

One truth visionaries must realize is that everyone becomes discouraged. It hits everyone, like death and taxes. Even the apostle Paul, the epitome of visionary leaders (see Eph. 3:20), experienced discouragement (2 Tim. 4:9–18). With discouragement, it is not a question of *if* but *when*.

This awareness can give a leader hope when discouragement strikes. He realizes that he is no different from anyone else. Moses, David, Paul, Luther, and many others have walked where he walks, treading knee-deep in the waters of discouragement. Obviously Paul spoke from experience when in 1 Corinthians 10:13 he wrote, "No temptation has overtaken you but such as is common to man." Certainly discouragement would be included under the broad category of temptation.

Not only did these leaders experience discouragement, but they also survived it. They lived to see another day. If they survived it, there is no reason to think we will not survive it as well. Perhaps the more important issue for leaders who are responsible for implementing dreams is not *if* they will survive it but *how* they survive it. Will they come through it with their vision still intact, or will it die?

Remember the Lord

Remember the Lord in times of intense discouragement, especially when it comes from fear. Nehemiah implemented this practice when he said to his people, "Do not be afraid of them; remember the Lord who is great and awesome, and fight for your brothers, your sons, your daughters, your wives and your houses" (Neh. 4:14). I believe that what Nehemiah had in mind here is the fact that in times of intense discouragement we forget about God because we become so focused on ourselves and our own difficult circumstances. We have to be reminded of God and the truth of his awesome goodness and greatness and that we have a good God who is on our side in the midst of our discouragement. We need to remember this in light of three contexts: God's past, present, and future goodness.

GOD'S PAST GOODNESS

God has demonstrated his awesome goodness to us in the past. It is most helpful, especially in times of discouragement, to pause and count all of God's past blessings in our lives. We can begin with the ultimate in blessings, our conversion to Christ and all that is associated with that life-changing event. But that is only the beginning. He continues to pour out his blessings on us in answered prayers, special friends, physical safety, good health, and many other ways.

GOD'S PRESENT GOODNESS

God continues to demonstrate his goodness in the present, particularly in the blessing of his special abiding presence in our lives. In Hebrews 13:5–6 the writer says, "Make sure that your character is free from the love of money, being content with what you have; for He Himself has said, 'I will never desert you, nor will I ever forsake you,' so that we confidently say, 'The Lord is my helper, I will not be afraid. What will man do to me?'"

According to the New Testament, this is a promise for all believers since the cross. However, in the Old Testament it was a special promise to God's visionary leaders, such as Moses and Joshua (Josh. 1:5, 9). In the midst of our present discouragement and difficulty, when we may have even forgotten God, he has not forgotten or abandoned us. He will never leave nor forsake us, and we will never experience discouragement and difficulty alone.

GOD'S FUTURE GOODNESS

God will not cease to pour out his goodness in the future. Because he will not abandon us, even when we leave him, Paul says, we cannot be separated from the love of Christ in our eternal state (Rom. 8:35–39). He concludes in verse 37, "But in all these things we overwhelmingly conquer through Him who loves us." Regardless of our circumstances, Paul says, we can view ourselves as conquerors in light of our position in Christ. Therefore, no matter what happens or how discouraged we may become, ultimately we win.

Ask God for Strength

Pray and ask God for the strength necessary to overcome the discouragement. In the Old Testament, Nehemiah prayed in the midst of the attempts of his enemies to discourage him and his people from the vision. He told God, "For all of them were trying to frighten us, thinking, 'They will become discouraged with the work and it will not be done.' But now, O God, strengthen my hands" (Neh. 6:9).

But what does that mean? How did God strengthen Nehemiah? David, who was no stranger to discouragement, offered a similar prayer in Psalm 138. In this thanksgiving psalm, God answered his prayer by strengthening his soul, which resulted in special boldness or courage, for he said, "On the day I called, You answered me; You made me bold with strength in my soul" (v. 3). Nehemiah's reference to his hands was probably a figure of speech for the work of his hands. He asked God in the midst of his discouraging circumstances to give him boldness or courage as he was about the business of leading his people in the rebuilding of the wall.

The New Testament equivalent to Nehemiah 6:9 is found in 2 Timothy 4:17. Paul was discouraged because many of his friends had abandoned him (vv. 10, 16), his enemies were attacking him (vv. 14–15), he was in jail, and his death was imminent (vv. 6–7). After detailing all this, he gave the solution for his discouragement: "But the Lord stood with me and strengthened me, so that through me the proclamation might be fully accomplished, and that all the Gentiles might hear; and I was rescued out of the lion's mouth."

Paul, like Nehemiah and David, received from God an infusion of strength necessary to accomplish his vision. Here Paul's vision was the proclamation of the gospel to the Gentiles that they might be saved (in essence the Great Commission).

Hang Tough

Visionary leaders must not give up on their visions in discouraging situations. They must hang tough; they must not be quick to quit. It is critical that they not let the light from their churches go out in their ministry communities (Matt. 5:14). Discouragement hits us emotionally much like a blow to the solar plexus; it knocks the emotional wind out of us. The result is that while we are down for the count, we are greatly tempted to give up on our dreams for God and not get up.

Rather than throw in the towel, God wants us to come up fighting. A great example of this tenacity is Nehemiah's leadership throughout his book. Nehemiah was a fighter, as seen in Nehemiah 4:14, where he not only challenges his people to remember the Lord but also adds, "and fight for your brothers, your sons, your daughters, your wives and your houses."

The apostle Paul was also a fighter and a finisher. At the end of his life he uses the metaphor of the boxer and runner: "I have fought the good fight, I have finished the course, I have kept the faith" (2 Tim. 4:7). And perhaps the motivation behind these metaphors is the hope found in 1 Corinthians 10:13 where he says, "No temptation has overtaken you but such as is common to man; and God is faithful, who will not allow you to be tempted beyond what you are able, but with the temptation will provide the way of escape also, so that you will be able to endure it." Therefore, we need to be patient and hang tough and not quit, because God says we can endure it.

I stated earlier in this chapter that overwhelming discouragement has eliminated many leaders from ministry. I advise that the visionary leader not make any major decisions, such as leaving a ministry, while discouraged. We must keep in mind that we are not in the right frame of mind when we are discouraged and possibly depressed. Our decisions, whether big or small, will be skewed and based on our circumstances, which are not good. Would we have made the same decision when encouraged? It is best to wait until we have applied some of the principles of this chapter and are in a better frame of mind before we make any major life-affecting decisions.

No matter how important or how high a person's leadership position in an organization, he is human and will fail on occasion. This means that sometime he may allow discouragement to get the best of him and give up and quit. The problem is that quitting only makes matters worse and adds guilt to the discouragement. But all is not lost. God has made provision for his people's failures at the cross of Christ and offers his forgiveness. John wrote, "If we confess our sins, He is faithful and righteous to forgive us our sins and to cleanse us from all unrighteousness" (1 John 1:9). David wrote in Psalm 32:5, "I acknowledged my sin to You, and my iniquity I did not hide; I said, 'I will confess my transgressions to the LORD'; and You forgave the guilt of my sin." We all must confess our failures to our forgiving, loving God and experience his forgiveness. Then we take back our towel, climb back in the ring, and continue the fight.

While God is quick to forgive, people may not be, and it is not always possible or wise to continue in the same ministry. Things that are said and done in the midst of discouragement often run deep emotionally and affect others in leaders' families, such as a spouse or children. They may never heal while in the same ministry or take so long to heal that it is best to move to a new ministry organization with a new team of people. This may mean that the visionary leader must settle for a position other than primary leader for a period of time until he proves himself again.

Encourage Others

Visionary leaders should make a point of encouraging others. Paul issues a general exhortation to those in the church at Thessalonica to encourage one another (1 Thess. 5:11). In Hebrews 3:13, the writer does the same to those who were tempted to fall away from the living God. On several occasions Paul specifically sent certain leaders to encourage the saints. He sent Timothy to Thessalonica so that he might strengthen and encourage them in their faith (3:2). He sent Tychicus to the believers at Colossae to update them on Paul's circumstances and to encourage their hearts (Col. 4:7–8).

Visionary leaders experience discouragement only at certain times, not all the time, so they know and understand what it is like for other leaders to go through difficult, discouraging times in their lives and ministries. Like Barnabas in Acts 11:22–23, an important aspect of their own ministries is to look for and seek to encourage other leaders who become discouraged and are ready to quit. In short, be an encourager.

Spend Time with Visionaries

Visionaries prevent discouragement in their lives by regularly exposing themselves to other visionary people and visionary material. Encouragement is infectious, making it important for visionary leaders to seek out one another's company and stay abreast of what others are doing in their ministries. Proverbs 27:17 says, "Iron sharpens iron, so one man sharpens another." I have several suggestions for how this can happen.

INDIVIDUAL MEETINGS

First, visionary leaders can seek out other leaders in ministries similar to theirs or possibly ones that are different. Pastors may want to meet with pastors, and parachurch leaders with parachurch leaders. This is because their ministries may have so much in common that they find it a "sharpening" experience when they get together. But it can be most beneficial to meet with those who lead in other organizations as well. Pastors can learn much from parachurch leaders, and both can learn from those who are leading in the business world.

Group Meetings

Another suggestion is for leaders to meet in groups. I meet once a month with a group of visionaries consisting of pastors and parachurch leaders from several different denominations. What we all have in common is a desire to be on the cutting edge of the Great Commission ministry. Our agenda varies from a review of the latest Christian or secular book on leadership to bringing in an outside specialist on some pertinent topic.

Pastors Conferences

Attend pastors conferences sponsored by churches that are led by strong visionaries. An excellent conference is the Global Leadership Summit that is put on by the Willow Creek Association. This conference takes place annually, and the number of people who can attend each conference is limited.

MP3s and Podcasts

Take advantage of recorded materials from various organizations that are on the cutting edge. Many have informative materials available on MP3s and podcasts.

Literature

Read broadly in areas related to leadership and creativity. Every good visionary leader is a reader. An increasing number of good Christian books on creative leadership are being published. Most Christian publishers will provide a catalog on request.

> **HOW TO SPEND TIME WITH VISIONARIES**
> - Meet with visionaries individually.
> - Meet with visionaries in groups.
> - Attend visionary pastors conferences.
> - View visionary podcasts.
> - Read visionary literature.

But innovative Christian leaders read good books on business as well. Tom Peters has made an excellent contribution to innovative leadership through several provocative, challenging books and videos (tompeters.com). Joel Arthur Barker has written a book and produced a video on paradigms and another video on vision (joel barker.com). I have found that a publisher of excellent works on business leadership and management is Jossey-Bass. Go online to view their catalog.

Another creative and challenging read is the magazine *Fast Company*. Check out their website (www.fastcompany.com).

Communicate with Vision Adversaries

Visionary leaders will encounter visionary vampires, vultures, and firemen who come into their ministries and discourage them. Dealing with fellow believers who oppose changes, for whatever reason, can be challenging and requires tact, understanding, wisdom, and patience. Following are some suggested steps.

MEET IN PRIVATE

The leader must arrange to meet with the vision adversary, preferably in private. This is the spirit of the Scriptures according to such passages as Matthew 5:23–24 and 18:15. Meeting privately allows the leader to determine if in fact there are any differences, get the parties to deal with their differences, and attempt to resolve the differences without unnecessary publicity for the individual or ministry.

IDENTIFY THE PROBLEM

Try to determine the nature of the problem. Most often it is a difference in philosophy or personality, a sin, or a combination thereof.

A philosophical difference between two people can be a problem. I would include under philosophy such matters as a different vision, a different philosophy of ministry, a preference for the status quo, and a different interpretation of Scripture. Usually these are differences of opinion that can be held by two reasonably mature Christians without involving sin on either side. It is important that the two people spend some time together trying to air out their differences and arrive at a consensus of opinion in a spirit of love and cooperation. If the person who differs with the ministry leader is also a leader, then a decision will have to be made as to whether that person should stay with the ministry or pursue something that is closer to his philosophy in another ministry.

A problem can be a difference in personality. A general rule is that those with similar personalities get along better than those with differing personalities. Again, it is important that the people involved get together to try to understand one another. God has designed us with different temperaments but with the ability to work together as a team to accomplish a particular vision. Each personality provides an important, necessary ingredient (1 Cor. 12:12–31).

In most cases, when a team of relatively mature people who understand the importance of their differences get together to accomplish the same dream, they learn to appreciate the gifts and abilities of the others and value their input. However, if they are unable to resolve their differences, it is hopefully not a problem with the primary leader and his maturity. Assuming this is the case and the other person is also a leader in the organization, it is probably best for the ministry that the other person leave the organization.

Possibly a problem is due to sin. Some people in ministry organizations are well-intentioned troublemakers. They work their way up through the ranks of a ministry organization until they reach a leadership position. They appear to be loyal to the ministry and are very faithful to it. In the church they are people who carry a Bible and are present at all the meetings of the church. They give regularly and show up on church workdays (which in some churches is equated with spirituality). But these people have a different vision with a different agenda.

They manifest themselves through their constant opposition to the visionary leader and the vision, and it becomes obvious that he will not be able to lead them. This is because ultimately they, like Diotrephes in 3 John 9, want to control the organization. They do not want the official title that goes with the primary leadership position, such as president or pastor. They are perfectly willing to let someone else have the title as long as they are the ones who call the shots.

Their strategy may involve recruiting and lining up others in the organization behind them and their agenda. These other people are probably dissidents as well who do not like the direction of the ministry organization. These individuals will seek to get what they want through innuendo, spreading false or questionable rumors, and encouraging factions in the organization. They hope to divide and conquer, for if they get enough people on their side, they will gain the control they desire to accomplish their ends. I wish this were not the case, but I have been in ministry long enough to know better. I call this the dark side of ministry.

What can a visionary leader do in a situation like this? A lot depends on whether this leader is already in power. If he is called to a ministry as the point person, it is always wise to try to determine if someone is already in power who might oppose him. If the person who was interim leader is still on the scene, the person who is considering the appointment should spend some time with him, expecting that the conversation will reveal either subtly or blatantly where the interim leader stands. It is best not to take a position in an organization like this in the first place. The leader who is not aware of the situation and winds up in an untenable situation may have to resign.

If the leader is already in the point position of a ministry and one of these individuals comes along, the point person must deal with him or her as soon as possible before it is too late. To ignore these people can cost a person his ministry. In Romans 16:17 Paul warns,

"Now I urge you, brethren, keep your eye on those who cause dissensions and hindrances contrary to the teaching which you learned, and turn away from them." Again, in Titus 3:10–11, he advises, "Reject a factious man after a first and second warning, knowing that such a man is perverted and is sinning, being self-condemned." If the person involved has become somewhat rooted in the ministry, then most likely it will be necessary to implement the disciplinary procedures according to Matthew 18:15–20.

RESOLVE THE PROBLEM

Finally, leaders should attempt to resolve any problems. Unresolved personal problems, whether in a ministry, a marriage, or any other relationship, have a way of piling up and coming back to them later in their ministries. Scripture commands us to resolve our differences (Matt. 5:24; 18:15). If the other party responds favorably, then we have won back a brother or sister. If that person does not respond, then, as in the worse-case scenario above, he must be disciplined.

> **HOW TO COMMUNICATE WITH VISION ADVERSARIES**
> - Meet with them in private.
> - Identify the problem.
> - Attempt to resolve the problem.

How to Beat Discouragement

There are seven biblical truths that summarize how leaders may fend off discouragement:

1. Recognize that discouragement is universal (2 Tim. 4:9–18).
2. Remember the Lord (Neh. 4:14).
3. Ask God for strength (Neh. 6:9).
4. Hang tough (Neh. 4:14; 2 Tim. 4:7).
5. Encourage others (1 Thess. 5:11).

6. Spend time with visionaries (Prov. 27:17).

7. Communicate with vision adversaries (Matt. 18:15).

Questions for Reflection and Discussion

1. Are you often discouraged in your ministry? Where would you place discouragement in your list of major ministry problems? Is it your main problem?

2. What are the sources of your discouragement? Do you face any vision vampires, vultures, or firemen? If so, who are they?

3. Do you face any other sources of discouragement, such as failure, fear, fatigue, or frustration? Which one(s)?

4. Can you pin your discouragement down to any one particular obstacle or combination of obstacles? You might find it helpful to express this and your feelings by writing them on paper or in your journal.

5. Check the behaviors you believe might turn your discouragement into encouragement. Be sure to put them into practice now and whenever you feel discouraged.

    ___ Recognize that discouragement is universal.

    ___ Remember the Lord.

    ___ Ask God for strength.

    ___ Hang tough.

    ___ Encourage others.

    ___ Spend time with visionaries and their materials.

    ___ Communicate with vision adversaries.

Appendix

Vision Statements

Moses's Vision
  Deuteronomy 8:7–10

Northwood Community Church
  Dallas, Texas

Lakeview Community Church
  Cedar Hill, Texas

River City Community Church
  Louisville, Kentucky

Saddleback Valley Community Church
  Mission Viejo, California

Crossroads Community Church
  Mansfield, Ohio

Clear Creek Community Church
  Houston, Texas

Willow Creek Community Church
  South Barrington, Illinois

Moses's Vision

"For the LORD your God is bringing you into a good land—a land with streams and pools of water, with springs flowing in the valleys and hills; a land with wheat and barley, vines and fig trees, pomegranates, olive oil and honey; a land where bread will not be scarce and you will lack nothing; a land where the rocks are iron and you can dig copper out of the hills."

Deuteronomy 8:7–10

Northwood Community Church
Dallas, Texas

Vision is not about reality or what is. Vision is all about our dreams and aspirations or what could be.

At Northwood Community Church, we envision our sharing the good news of Christ's death and resurrection with thousands of unchurched friends and people in the metroplex, many of whom accept him as Savior.

We envision developing all our people—new believers as well as established believers—into fully functioning followers of Christ through people-friendly worship services, Sunday school, special events, and most important, small groups.

We envision becoming a church of small groups where our people model biblical community: a safe place where we accept one another and are accepted, love and are loved, shepherd and are shepherded, encourage and are encouraged, forgive and are forgiven, and serve and are served.

We envision helping all our people—youth as well as adults—to discover their divine designs so that they are equipped to serve Christ effectively in some ministry either within or outside our church. Our goal is that every member be a minister.

We envision welcoming numerous members into our body who are excited about Christ, experience healing in their family relationships and marriages, and grow together in love.

We envision recruiting, training, and sending out many of our members as missionaries, church planters, and church workers all over the world. We also see a number of our people pursuing short-term missions service in various countries. We envision planting a church in America or abroad every two years.

We envision a larger facility that will accommodate our growth and be accessible to all the metroplex. This facility will provide ample room for Sunday school, small groups, Bible study, prayer, and other meetings. While we do not believe that "bigger is better," numerical growth is a by-product of effective evangelism. Thus, we desire to grow as God prospers us and uses us to reach a lost and dying world.

This is our dream—our vision about what could be!

Aubrey Malphurs
January 1997

Lakeview Community Church
Cedar Hill, Texas

Our comprehensive purpose is to honor our Lord and Savior, Jesus Christ, by carrying out his command to make disciples of all nations (Matthew 28:19–20). Specifically, we believe God has called us to focus on reaching those in Cedar Hill and the surrounding areas who do not regularly attend any church.

In order to accomplish this, Lakeview Community Church will be an equipping center where every Christian can be developed to his or her full potential for ministry. This development will come through:

a) creative, inspiring worship;

b) teaching that is biblical and relevant to life;

c) vital, supportive fellowship; and

d) opportunities for outreach into the community in service and evangelism.

As a result, the Cedar Hill area will be different in ten to fifteen years, with the Christian influence being increasingly felt in homes, businesses, education, and politics. We further intend to multiply our worldwide ministry by planting churches, by preparing our people for leadership roles in vocational ministries and parachurch groups, by sending out missionaries, and by becoming a resource center and model for Texas and the nation.

River City Community Church
Louisville, Kentucky

WE SEE . . .

. . . the light of truth cutting through the darkness!
At River City, we will seek to lead irreligious people from the darkness of separation from God to a relationship with Him by proclaiming clearly and often the truth of eternal life in Jesus Christ. Corporately, we will provide a Sunday morning service that is exciting, interesting, and friendly. We will also have outreach events such as concerts, block parties, sports, and festivals. Individually, the mature, trained followers of Christ will reach out to friends, family, and neighbors.

WE SENSE . . .

. . . the aroma of freedom from a selfish lifestyle!
At River City, believers are encouraged to shed the shackles of harmful and selfish behavior and enjoy the freedom of following Christ. They understand the characteristics of a fully-functioning follower and are challenged to become one. In formal teaching times and small groups, believers find the means for learning how to study the Word, pray to God, share their faith, and practice hospitality.

WE HEAR . . .

. . . the sound of laughter breaking down the walls of silence!

At River City, we will be a family that calls people from the loneliness of isolation to the joy of relationships. We will seek to know, serve, encourage, challenge, and love one another. We will welcome all people regardless of race, sex, or history into our family, just as God has welcomed believers into His family by His grace. We will not be afraid to laugh or have fun.

WE FEEL . . .

. . . the strength of a loving hand training us to serve!

At River City, men and women will receive further training in order to become leaders who make disciples. As a result of our worship, evangelism, assimilation, and leadership training, we will become a church of ministers that carries out the Great Commission, meets the needs of one another, builds safer communities, and glorifies the name of Jesus Christ in the city of Louisville, Kentucky.

Saddleback Valley Community Church
Mission Viejo, California

It is the dream of a place where the hurting, the depressed, the frustrated, and the confused can find love, acceptance, help, hope, forgiveness, guidance, and encouragement.

It is the dream of sharing the Good News of Jesus Christ with the hundreds of thousands of residents in south Orange County.

It is the dream of welcoming 20,000 members into the fellowship of our church family—loving, learning, laughing, and living in harmony together.

It is the dream of developing people to spiritual maturity through Bible studies, small groups, seminars, retreats, and a Bible school for our members.

It is the dream of equipping every believer for a significant ministry by helping them discover the gifts and talents God gave them.

It is the dream of sending out hundreds of career missionaries and church workers all around the world, and empowering every member for a personal life mission in the world. It is the dream of sending our members by the thousands on short-term mission projects to every continent. It is the dream of starting at least one new daughter church every year.

It is the dream of at least fifty acres of land, on which will be built a regional church for south Orange County—with beautiful, yet simple facilities including a worship center seating thousands, a counseling and prayer center, classrooms for Bible studies and training lay ministers, and a recreation area. All of this will be designed to minister to the total person—spiritually, emotionally, physically, and socially—and set in a peaceful inspiring garden landscape.

I stand before you this day and state in confident assurance that these dreams will become reality. Why? Because they are inspired by God!

Crossroads Community Church
Mansfield, Ohio

The Vision

The writer of Proverbs wrote, "Where there is no vision the people perish" (29:18). At Crossroads, it is our desire that you catch the vision God has given us, that you begin to visualize the invisible. We have worked hard at defining our vision so that it is clear, challenging, and concise. It is our desire that you clearly see the future of the ministry—what it can be and what it must be. But most importantly, we want you to capture the concept of our vision so that it will capture you and provide a foundation for your personal ministry with us at Crossroads.

In part, the vision of Crossroads Community Church is to become a biblically functioning community. This will become clear as you continue through the notebook. However, our complete vision statement more specifically defines our desires.

Crossroads Vision Statement

The vision of Crossroads Community Church is to creatively implement the Great Commission to build a growing community of churches around the perimeter of Mansfield by planting culturally relevant churches every three years that are committed to dynamic worship of God while extending His transforming grace to reach the unchurched community.

There are five key phrases that outline our vision. They represent the core of our vision and are essential for evaluating, redefining, and sharpening our focus. The five key phrases are:

CREATIVELY IMPLEMENT THE GREAT COMMISSION

Jesus summarized his purpose for being on earth in Luke 19:10. He said, "For the Son of man is come to seek and to save that which was lost." In his final instructions he made the purposes of the church clear. "Go and make disciples of all nations, baptizing them in the name of the Father and of the Son and of the Holy Spirit, and teaching them to obey everything I have commanded you" (Matt. 28:19–20). Therefore, our vision includes pursuing the lost in the most culturally relevant format. This includes implementing Christ's commission in both an innovative and creative manner to the unchurched of our community.

BUILD A GROWING COMMUNITY OF CHURCHES

Unchurched people are nine times more likely to come to a new church rather than an older, established church (*Christianity Today*). We feel that the best means of impacting our area with the transforming message of Christ is to plant culturally relevant churches, like Crossroads, around our community. For us, this means starting a new church every three years in strategic locations so as to build a perimeter of churches around the city.

COMMITTED TO DYNAMIC WORSHIP

Because our vision is to extend the transforming grace of Jesus Christ, we believe that the most fundamental relationship people can have is an active, living relationship with God through Jesus Christ His Son (John 10:10; Romans 6:23). Our worship services reflect this by promoting creative, inspiring, and authentic worship which demonstrates that God is living and active in this generation; therefore, the most contemporary medium is used to express our worship.

EXTENDING HIS TRANSFORMING GRACE

By the grace of God, the city of Mansfield will be a changed community in 10 to 15 years, due to the influence of the Spirit of God through the lives of our people who are devoted to extending the transforming grace of Jesus Christ. It is our vision that the members of Crossroads will take Christ into homes, marketplaces, political arenas, and educational settings. Our Sunday morning service reflects our vision by being a safe place for Crossroads members to bring their friends, relatives, and co-workers. In other words, Crossroads is a safe place to hear a dangerous message.

REACH THE UNCHURCHED

Finally, our vision includes the intentional pursuit of reaching those who have stopped attending, or have never attended, a church. In other words, those who have not experienced God's transforming grace.

Placing a vision in print is somewhat like attempting to hold water in your hand. It is nearly impossible! A vision is something that is caught rather than taught. It has been described as a mental picture of the future which finds its realization in the hands of the one who owns the vision. It is our desire that the Crossroads vision becomes your vision; something you "own" and take great pride in seeing fulfilled. In essence, our vision is not something that you can see, but something you must be.

Clear Creek Community Church
Houston, Texas

Vision for Children's Ministry

We envision children waking up parents on Sunday morning excited to go to church.

We see lots of smiles, glad to be in a place of belonging, welcomed again by a familiar face. We see the fright of first time melted by an extra caring touch and loneliness replaced with laughter. We see motivated volunteers, passionate about being with kids, gifted to teach, serve, and shepherd.

We see a facility which is "kid focused" that will facilitate learning and having fun for hundreds of kids. We see a clean and attractive environment where excellence and creativity are immediately noticed.

We see concerned moms relieved as they drop off their children, and dads without distraction, engaged in the service. We envision a security process which builds confidence with parents.

We see physical care—babies being cuddled and crawlers being chased. We sense a foundation being laid where Sunday morning is an experience of God's love for the youngest baby to the oldest child, a time when seeds of faith can be planted and nurtured.

We hear cheers of older kids and feel fun in the air as hundreds of kids celebrate and sing of the goodness of God; we hear the quietness of prayer. We envision the stories of the Bible told in creative ways. We see the look of conviction as the gospel penetrates a child's heart. We see caring adults leading discussion and listening during small group time. We dream of kids carrying Bibles and bringing friends.

We see whole families growing closer to God and each other through programs to motivate and equip parents.

In the next five years, we envision hundreds of kids choosing to be baptized and building a faith foundation that will lead to a lifetime of full devotion to Christ and multiplication of kingdom impact.

Will Mancini
Clear Creek Community Church

Willow Creek Community Church
South Barrington, Illinois

Vision Night '96
Bill Hybels

Someone was introducing me at a conference not long ago and they introduced me as the senior pastor of the church that had just completed the most astonishing twenty-year ministry run in modern church history. And that person went on describing the various ways that Willow has made contributions to this community and the nation and the world, and I was all embarrassed wishing he would sort of bring it to a close. And then he said to the crowd that he was introducing me to, he said sort of half jokingly, "We are all wondering tonight, what is Willow Creek going to do for an encore? What is ahead? Is it going to fizzle? Is it going to have another run?" And then he said these words, "And you can bet we will all be watching."

I had sensed that there are a lot of folks inside and outside this church who have been waiting and who are going to be watching what we do in this next season of ministry. For the last several years we have been meeting in leadership teams and we have been asking each other, "Where are we going?" "What is next?" And this has floated around the elders, the staff, the management team, board, pilot groups throughout the church, "Where from here?"

We decided not to try to look twenty years out; that was just a ridiculous prospect. Not even ten years out, but what in the reasonable, the foreseeable future, the next five-year run. And as we have been talking about this, we know five years from now, if the Lord does not return, we know that probably the land will still be like it is and the buildings will still be standing and the gates will still be here, but the question that we have been asking is, "What will the church be like?" "What will this church be like five years from now?" "It is going to be like something. What is it going to be like?"

But then we have refined the question and asked, I think the best question, "What would God love for Willow Creek to look like five years from now?" "What would God like us to look like five years from now?" "What values does God want us to pay special attention to?" "What goals should we set?" "What programs should be launched?" "What should we really focus on?" So after hundreds of hours of prayer and interaction and review, I am going to give you just three great big ideas that the whole vision for the next five years sort of falls out under. Three values that we have to lift up powerfully and live out passionately, and the first one is going to come up on the side screen.

Strategic Focus #1

We feel we need to reach an ever increasing percentage of the Chicagoland area with the gospel message. This one came quickly and it came unanimously. All of us in leadership feel absolutely certain that the next five years must be an all-out full court press to communicate the message of salvation to this community and the greater Chicagoland area. Simply put, friends, we believe God is saying to us as a church, you are not finished yet. We feel that God is saying there are thousands and thousands of lost people who matter to Him, who are not in His family yet, and we feel that God is saying that He is counting on the witness of this church to just burn brightly, brighter than ever in the next five years. To be a beacon of hope to people who are lost and facing a Christless eternity. We feel that God is saying, cast the gospel message out there, and be free with it and even be reckless with it, because there are lots of folks who need to hear who haven't heard it yet.

I fly into Chicago at night on a fairly regular basis and I look out the window and I see the shimmering lights of our city, and I am often reminded of the words of Jesus, who looked over a metropolitan area one time and he started crying because he said there are just a lot of wandering sheep down there without a shepherd, without a Savior. There are a lot of lost folks there. And I think that as God looks at our immediate community and the greater Chicagoland area, that God weeps as well. There is lots of, lots of work to be done. And again, we just feel with great clarity that the next five years we need to enter into a time where fruit will be born and where hearts will be redeemed, where lives will be transformed, and where people will turn from sin toward repentance and Jesus Christ in record numbers.

And so as of tonight, the starting gun goes off and we charge into a future that is going to be marked with evangelistic intensity. And I for one just can't wait. It was evangelistic intensity that fueled the launching of this church. We used to pray in small groups in the basement of South Park Church when we were just a youth group before this church. We used to fast and pray for our friends who were outside the faith. And when we started this church, we felt so strongly about it, as you know, we sold tomatoes door to door to just raise enough money to launch the first service so we could pass the gospel out, so somebody who needed to hear it would hear it and come to faith. We're going to get back to that kind of intensity.

This evangelistic intensity will be expressed first and foremost in each one of our lives, all of us who are of the core of Willow Creek here at New Community, because we are all going to receive a new round of training and instruction. How to become contagious Christians ourselves. It doesn't start with me making some big statement about evangelistic intensity. The kingdom of God advances one life at a time. It happens when your heart is changed and you see lost people as Christ sees lost people. And you understand that there is a heaven and that there is a hell and real people go there forever, and you are called as I am called in our individual lives to love lost people and to build relationships with them, and when the opportunity presents itself to share a bold witness for Christ to them and then invite them to our seekers services as God gives us power and unction to do them here on weekends. But friends, as we announce the new evangelistic intensity, it begins in your heart.

Now the ironic thing is that the last couple years this church and particularly through the association has developed the premier evangelistic training course in the Western world. It is called *Becoming a Contagious Christian* and just out of the thousands and thousands of Christ followers in this church there are only 185 people or so who have been through this new training course. And so over the next five years we are going to set as an objective that every single person who considers himself a Christian here at Willow Creek is going to go through the Contagious Christianity course where we learn and relearn and get sharpened and resharpened how to look at a lost world. And how to live in vital union with Christ, such that we are salt with savor, and salt that has proximity to that which it is trying to affect. And where we have evangelistic impact in our individual lives. So we are going to start with us, all receiving additional training.

And then beyond that, we are going to turn up the thermostat at weekend services. I mean, we are just going to do a whole lot more presentations of the gospel, series for seekers. Series like reasons to believe. Lots of outreach kinds of things. We are probably going to have to offer a fourth weekend service. We don't know if it will be on Saturday or on Sunday; we are not sure yet. We are going to work the details out on that later. But you will sense that more and more the evangelistic thermostat of our weekend services will go up.

Because I kind of knew this was coming, just the last couple of weeks when I have been talking about monetary stuff, you notice that I have been ending the messages with a strong gospel approach. This last weekend at one of the services I said, look, we have talked a little bit about moving toward financial freedom. Some of you are still in spiritual bondage, and every opportunity I get, and Lee who spells me most of the time at the weekend, we are just going to pledge to you that we are going to look for every way we can to make the gospel message come alive more and more at our weekend services so that you can just invite the friends that you are witnessing to, to come here, and we will help you lead them to Christ.

Another thing that we are going to do is stress throughout all of the small groups—ten thousand people are in small groups in this church—and we are going to pick up that empty chair, that open chair, and we are going to say for God's sake, fill it. For the sake of lost people, fill it. With ten thousand people in small groups, if all of us would just invite over the course of the next twelve months or twenty-four months, one lost person to join our small group, just think ten thousand folks can spend eternity in heaven. If all of us in groups would just invite somebody in. Friends, this would be just an unbelievable thing, wouldn't it? We are going to say, start praying to fill that open chair. Make it a group goal. Commit yourself to it. Watch what God does.

We are going to launch Access as an outreach ministry. It has been building a core for the last year or so, but it is going to be an outreach ministry in just a little while. Another thing that we are going to do is go back to the days when we had evangelistic outreach concerts. And when we had pre-evangelistic outreach concerts. Another that I get to announce yet tonight is just in the short-term future coming up here in a few weeks we are going to do the Choice again. It is just a unanimous decision. We are going to have multiple presentations of it. If you are new around here, it is one of the most powerful presentations of the last days of the ministry of Christ, Good Friday, and Easter. We have done it twice before in years past. It is powerful. Lost people respond to Christ when they are invited to it. We want to fill this place eight or ten times with people that you invite. And we will do our best to put it on in a way that will just honor Christ. But again we are going to do team evangelism. It is something that we can all do together. You do your part and the music/drama people will do their part. But we want to see thousands of folks be touched with the power of the gospel.

Then we will go to Easter, which will be an outreach-oriented Easter service. The post-Easter series is one that I am working on right now that will be just ideal for you to invite friends to. So we are just going to hit the ground running on this. A verse that just keeps welling up in my heart these days is Romans 1:16: "For I am not ashamed of the gospel of Christ, it is the power of God unto salvation." It is what has to be cast out there. The gospel still changes hearts and lives. That is why you are in here tonight, because someone told you that Christ died for sinners and you believed it and it changed your heart. That message is going to go out with frequency and with power like never before.

There is another thing that we are going to do because we want to reach the Chicagoland area. We looked way down the road and got within a hair's breadth of committing ourselves to starting a couple satellite churches. But, friends, at the eleventh hour and fifty-ninth minute, and I am not kidding you, we came dangerously close, right at the end God used one particular individual on our leadership team to say hang on, back it up. Let's take one long look at this again. Who did God make us to be? Who are the leaders of this church? How are they best gifted to have impact around the country and around the world? What is the best usage of the team that God has put together? So we went all the way back to zero and we started again. In the meantime, Jimmy Auto, president of our Willow Creek

211

Association, did some research and found out that there are somewhere between thirty and forty Willow Creek Association churches within a reasonable driving radius in the Chicagoland area. Thirty or forty association churches. And so we started brainstorming and we said, What if we at Willow put a special synergistic emphasis behind those thirty or forty churches and helped them become evangelistically intense, and said let's do that.

Instead of our assuming responsibility for one or two other churches, we could just lift the entire spiritual climate of the Chicagoland area through our existing organization of the association and put special emphasis into those thirty or forty pastors, and we just feel that it is the way God wants us to go. So we are going to work in tight synergy with those leaders.

To make sure that we are not just blowing smoke about this whole goal of evangelism, we have chosen a goal of having a weekend attendance of in excess of twenty thousand people in the next few years. I mean our goal is, we run about fifteen thousand right now, and we want to move that to twenty thousand in the next few years. And Lee Strobel has stepped up, and he has said that he is willing to be the point person, the champion of this stallion. And he will gather other leaders around it to make sure that the entire staff and all the leaders of the church are working together toward this goal.

But I will tell you, friends, a few weeks ago when we had a baptism up here, God did something in my heart. I barely made it through those two nights, because I think, I think it is because we have sort of been in neutral evangelistically the last couple of years because we have been doing infrastructure rebuilds. I was not meant to function in neutral evangelistically, I will tell you. It has been very difficult. I have been telling the staff, we have been in an unnatural mode through the last three years while we have been rebuilding stuff. I don't think I could have taken it another month or two. At that last baptism service was just person after person after person when I said, have you trusted Christ for the forgiveness of your sins? And they didn't just answer the way we told them to. We said to say yes or something like that. Folks, with tears streaming down their cheeks, they would say yes with all of my heart, yes, you don't know how glad I am that Christ has saved me. I just saw up close and personal again what happens to a human heart when Christ redeems it. And I just thought, that's it, no more neutral, no more neutral. Settle down. We are going, that's it. Okay? There are a hundred churches in neutral within a driving radius of this church. If you like neutral, go there. We are not going to be in neutral. Settle down. We are going that way. Let it be clear.

It took days of prayer for me to stay that restrained. I am celebrating a little personal victory that I kept my spirit under control on that one. Let's move onto the second large focus that we are going to be moving toward.

Strategic Focus #2

We are going to move the congregation of Christ followers toward community, spiritual maturity, and full participation within the life of the church. If we have learned anything in the past few years, it's that once a person trusts Christ, the challenge is not over but just beginning. Our mission statement has always been we are trying to turn irreligious people, not just into Christians, but into what? Say it, fully devoted followers. You didn't say it convincingly. Let's say it once more. We are trying to turn irreligious people into fully devoted followers of Christ. That's right.

What we are saying in the second major value is that in the next five years we would like to see huge progress in this church, in moving Christ followers into community, into spiritual maturity, and into full participation in the church. And we have a long way to go. Here is a staggering statistic that we should not be proud of. Right now 74 percent of people who attend our weekend services say that they are not connected in any meaningful fellowship. Almost 45 percent of the New Community, of you gathered here, are not in small groups yet. Listen, friends, God made your heart to yearn for community. You long to know and be known, to love and be loved, to serve and be served, to celebrate and be celebrated. You are not going to be fully whole in Christ until you experience community on a consistent basis.

When a few moments ago, Janice Yarrow, who has served faithfully as an elder for ten years, when she said she was going to transition off being an elder, but she is going to continue to be our small group leader, when she said she was willing to continue, I wanted to sing the Hallelujah Chorus because, when we meet together as elders first hour, we meet in her home and she fixes us a meal and she just shepherds us and she cares for us and she calls us during the week and says, how can I pray for you? Because I love you and I am committed to you, and I get notes from her and the other elders do too. And we enjoy community.

Our management team, we enjoy community. I have told you before, I am at a stage in my life where there are only two things that I want anymore really in life. I want to do God's bidding for my life with all of my heart, but I want to do it in the context of community. I want to do it with people, that I can be known and be known with, love and be loved by, serve and serve with, and they can celebrate me and I can celebrate them. Friends, the next five years are going to be wonderful years for all of you who are in community, and they are not going to be as wonderful as they could be for those of you who are not yet in community. So we are just committed to saying, anybody in isolation that is just unacceptable. We want to encourage you and move you and pull you toward community. We want to move you toward community.

We want to move toward spiritual maturity. John Hartford has just been trying so hard to get us to understand that there are certain practices, there are certain relationships, there are certain experiences that we need to have in order to move toward maturity in Christ. Some of you who have been around this church a long time—we like to say, I haven't been a Christian that long; we like to claim baby status. Friends, some of you are not babies anymore. Some of you were baby Christians fifteen years ago. You ought to be shaving by now. You can't claim just the milk stuff anymore. You are far past in chronological years, you know, the baby status thing. If you are a year or two or three old in Christ, that is one thing, you can claim you need some diapers yet. The rest of you, it is time that you take responsibility to moving toward fullness of spiritual maturity. And we are going to do everything in our power, mostly here at New Community through worship and through teaching and then in the small groups, to mature you in the faith. There is a whole new spiritual formation emphasis that is coming out up the pike that you are going to be hearing more about. But it is time for the immature to move toward maturity in a very intentional way.

And it also says here that we are going to move the congregation toward full participation within the life of the church. Friends, we have said it over and over again, if this Willow Creek is just a wonderful place to hang around, if you just want to be around a place where there is spiritual vitality where you can be fed, where you can worship, where you can hear great teaching, where you can just have your heart touched consistently week after week after week, then this is the place to hang around. But you don't want to stand before a Savior who shed His blood for you, you don't want to stand before Him someday and say I never committed myself to the body of Christ at Willow Creek, I never found my spiritual gift, I never put on a uniform and became a part of the serving core of the church. You don't want to have white, unstained, uncallused hands when you put your hand in the bloodstained hand with a hole in the middle of it. You don't want that to happen. And we are going to do everything in our power to move you out of nonparticipation toward participating in the body of Christ.

We are going to fire up the Network Ministry once again. In the next forty-five days you will have an opportunity to go into Network.

215

And this is just like Contagious Christianity, but it is about spiritual gifts. Over the next few years we want every single person who considers himself a core member here at Willow Creek to go through the Network program to find out anew or to have a refresher course on what your spiritual gift is. Some of you thought you knew four or five years ago, but then you never took action on it, you never found a place where you really fit, and where you feel like you are making a difference.

Friends, we are going to be relentless in challenging you to identify your spiritual gift and to get off dead center and to get in the game. Because if you are in community and if you are growing in personal spiritual maturity and if you are a full participating, serving member in the body of Christ, then this next five-year run is going to be a ball. But if you are standing on the sidelines or if you are sitting in the stands, then when we hit the objectives that we are all aiming for and when we are a completely different church, a much more God-glorifying and Christ-honoring church five years from now, and we have some huge celebration where we honor God in that regard, you'll have to sit on the sidelines and say I wasn't a part of that. You don't want to do that. This is your best shot at doing something wonderful with the next five years of your life.

We are all going to make house payments, and we are all going to try to raise our kids, and we are all going to do the mundane stuff that life just includes. What are you going to do that is great for eternity? What are you going to do that is great for the kingdom of God? What are you going to do that is going to make you feel proud when you stand before your Savior someday with some calluses on your hands saying I was a player. What are you going to do? Well again, we are going to move you relentlessly toward finding your spiritual gift and identifying it, developing it, taking responsibility on yourself to finding a place in the church where you can use that gift. And when you do, and you find a place of joyful service, you will just be so glad.

Now because we want to be very specific about these values, community, spiritual maturity, and full participation within the life of the church, we have set some specific target goals and they are aggressive and there are people taking responsibility in writing point on them. We want to see increased community. We want to move from ten thousand people in the small groups, over the next few years, this next five-year run, to twenty thousand people in small groups. The twenty thousand people who attend the weekend services, that was our first objective that Lee is going to champion—we say everyone who comes to weekend services, anyone who considers Willow Creek a part of their worshipping experience—we are going to try to move them toward participation in a small group. Russ Robinson, whom you saw on the stage here, is committing the next five years of his life to say I and my team will do everything we can do to pave the way, to train the leaders, to open the doors, to allow twenty thousand people to come into community. Friends, if we hit that goal, that is going to be one of the most exciting God-honoring goals I can imagine toward increased maturity.

John Ortburg has said, "I will give the next five years of my life toward having eight thousand people become regular worshippers and learners at the New Community." John said, "I will be the anchor teacher. I will direct the New Community. Have Joe and Deter and others lead us in worship." The goal is in the next five years, to fill this place to capacity on Wednesday and Thursday night so that we can just lift voices together and sing, "Shout to the Lord," and "Shine Jesus Shine," and "How Great Thou Art" and have eight thousand people regularly honoring God and learning together.

And also we have set a goal of having eight thousand participating members in this church. The highest that we have ever had, even under the old membership, was two thousand. We were never pleased with that. But we have a membership system now that we just believe it honors God. It is right out of the pages of Scripture.

It captures those five Gs, grace, growth, group, gifts, and good stewardship. These are things that every Christ follower wants to have true in his or her life.

So here is the deal. We are serving notice. Some of you a little while ago we said, stand if you are already participating members or if you fully intend on becoming one in 1996. Now there is a whole bunch of you that didn't stand. I am glad that you are here, but expect some heat. I am telling you, friends, expect some heat. This is going to be hard for me to say. It is going to be harder for you to hear. Write all the letters you want to write, and don't expect a response, because I am standing on this one, friends.

If you are unwilling, over time, to throw your hat in the ring and to say I am willing to get in the game and commit myself to the church that God has called me to, to be a responsible member of this place. If you are just resisting and you say I am not going to do it, I am just going to be a bystander, a fence sitter, someone on the sidelines, then here is what I want to say, sit in another church, because listen, friends, we need that seat opened up for someone who is going to come to Christ and someone who is going to get discipled and join a group and grow in full maturity and become a participating member here. Because listen, this is not about club membership, this is about redeeming the world.

There is a lost and dying world. And it is not going to be reached by folks who just sit on the sidelines. We have to turn a congregation into a mobilized army of people who in the name of Christ will become players and servers and prayers and givers to achieve the objective that God has in mind for us. So once again, those are hard words and I know some of you are going to be very mad at me, and you are going to say, I like to sit in that church down the block, and I like to sit in this church on this block, and I like to do a little of this and I like to do a little of that. Friends, the heat is going to get so high that you are going to have to make a decision sooner or later. And we just want you, if you want to be a full participating member, a server, a player in the church down the street, get there, go there, be a full player there, but we need to have full players here and we are just going to not back off that and we are going to head in that direction, as the strong sense of the leadership bodies of this church. So that is where we are going together.

STRATEGIC FOCUS #3

We are going to invest a greater percentage of our lives and our knowledge and our resources with those in our city, our nation, and our world. John 3:16, the most often quoted verse in the Scripture, says, For God so loved, what? The world. God so loved the world. The Great Commission. Jesus said, You go out into the world. You see, God always thinks globally; God acts globally; God loves globally; God redeems globally. His heart breaks for the hurting and the poor and the lost, globally. And God has made it abundantly clear to those of us in leadership over the last few years that these beautiful glass walls of this auditorium must never again be viewed as boundaries that hold back the explosive work of the Holy Spirit that is so obvious within these walls. We have the opportunity and even beyond that the responsibility in this new era, we have a responsibility to the world. And we are finally ready as leaders to stop playing down the extraordinary influence that God has given us as a church and we are ready to say, we will take on that responsibility, we will wear that mantle, humbly but seriously and intentionally. And by God's grace we will move out into the world and we will seek in the inner city, the Dominican Republic, and various places all around the world. We will seek to expand the kingdom of God regionally, nationally, and internationally.

This is just not about hype or rhetoric. We already have the infrastructures in place. We have been building them the last three or four years. We have community care ministries right here, a part of our own church here at Willow, that care for the poor and the suffering among us. Ministries such as the food pantry, fellowship housing, the benevolence ministry, the car ministry, and a dozen other ministries that already exist here. They are staffed up. There are volunteers in place for some of the positions. We need more volunteers, but we are prepared to start to bring a lot of compassion and relief and hope and help to the poor among us.

And then we have our international ministries department, and it is staffed and it is funded and it is ready to go. And they are targeting the inner city and certain emerging churches. And then we have the Willow Creek Association that is staffed, and it is working well. It has already linked up fourteen hundred churches around the world bringing renewal and rejuvenation to them. So I mean we are spooled up, we are ready to release more of our lives and our knowledge and our resources. And, friends, I have to tell you, the world is waiting; the world is hoping; the world is depending on those of us in this church to bring some help and some hope.

In just the last few months, I have visited many of the projects that we are involved in, in the inner city and other places around the world. Friends, I just want to say this to you, when you go, when you make the visits, when you roll up your sleeves, when you volunteer, when you see God at work amongst the poor, when you see God at work in a foreign culture, you see God at work on the other side of the world that we have been able to influence and help a little bit. I will just tell you, you will never be the same. And so, what we are setting as a target goal, we are setting as a goal that by the year 2000 there will be eight thousand of us per year who are participating in the giving of our lives, in our knowledge, in our resources to ministries outside Willow Creek. Be it through community care, through international ministries, or the Willow Creek Association.

Maybe some of these numbers start making some sense. We are saying we want to see twenty thousand folks at our weekend services, many who are seekers, who are coming to know Christ. And then all of those folks we want to become members of small groups so they are at least moved into community. And then we want to see eight thousand people worshipping and learning at the New Community, and eight thousand participating members and that represents the strong mobilized army, the core of Willow. And out of all of that eight thousand numbered group, we want to see every person in that group be involved on an annual basis at least once, going down into the inner city, and working side by side with someone who has only known hardship and tragedy. Or we want to get you onto an airplane to go to the Dominican Republic and help build a home for someone who has never had a home. Or we want to send you somewhere around the world where the association is putting on conferences, where you can help us put on conferences, be it in Germany, or Australia, or South Africa, or Brazil, or wherever we are being invited these days to go to try and bring help, and hope, and renewal to the church.

But, friends, this is a new day, and I for one am so grateful about this. Because for the last couple of years I have dealt with a lot of guilt. My heart and fundamental calling has always been to be the pastor here at Willow Creek, but every time I felt God leading me to speak to another group of churches or to a conference at some other place or in another nation, I felt guilty flying away from this church. Sensing that I am shirking my responsibilities here, and lots of times, hundreds of times, before I would land to where I was going to go speak I would just say, that is it. I have just got to stop doing this because I really have to just pay all of my attention back at Willow, what is happening inside the walls. And then I would get up and I would give a talk, and while I would be giving the talk there would be this incredible surge of the Holy Spirit that I could just feel. And the Holy Spirit would say this is part of what I want you to do and this is part of what I want other people in and around Willow to do as well. I want you to think wider and more globally. This is the way God thinks. This is the way I want you to think more.

I have had such terrible inner tension in my spirit about all of this. And when the leaders of this church in just the past few years came together and said, look, we are going to make it intentional that part of what we are about as a church from here on out, this next five-year run, is we are about investing a greater percentage of our lives, that means my life too, and our knowledge, and our resources with those in our city, in our nation, and our world. And I think as eight thousand of us participate in this grand adventure—John Burke on our management team is the person who is writing point on this—I will give the next five years of my life through international ministries, the association, and others. I will give the next five years of my life to involve eight thousand people a year in an experience like that. When that happens to you, it is going to fill you up so full that you are going to wonder why we ever thought less than globally. That is where we are headed in these next few years, and I am so glad we are.

The Willow Creek Association has as its goal to move from fourteen hundred churches that we are helping, that are a member of the association, to four thousand churches. And Jim Miato says, you know he is the president of the association, he is saying I will give the next five years of my life to try to move our core from fourteen hundred to four thousand churches. And that is an exciting venture.

But anyway, those three big emphases, that sort of crystallizes where we are going together. We are going to reach a greater percentage of our community with the gospel. We are going to move our Christ followers here toward community, maturity, and participation in the body of Christ, and we are going to invest more of ourselves, and our knowledge, and our resources, around our city and our nation and our world.

Now, friends, I have to say this in closing, we don't have a prayer of reaching these goals without you. I mean, we are not into grandiosity. This is not a few leaders in a room thinking these are great ideas, we think we can pull them off. We have a tremendous sense of humility and inadequacy surrounding each of these goals. But somehow, you know, we just feel that if every single person in this place said, that is it, I mean I will do the mundane stuff I have to do with my regular life but I am going to be a part of this great adventure. Here is the way I am thinking about it. Maybe this will help you. When we celebrated our twentieth anniversary, so many folks, hundreds and hundreds, wrote letters and said I would have given anything to be a founder. You all here tonight, I mean, you are here as the gun goes off for this five-year plan. You are founders in this five-year run. I mean, you are here.

There is a famous verse in the Old Testament book of Esther where a man of God says to Esther, maybe in the scheme of God you were appointed to live for just such a time as this. Do you know what I want to say to you? I don't think it is an accident that you are in a room tonight. I think the whole course of your life led up to a point where you would be saved and growing and enough of a Christ follower to be sitting in a room tonight with an expectant heart, excited about where your church is going. And I just want to say I think God appointed you for such a time as this and we need you. And I don't want to end this talk by saying, you know, let's have a big applause if you are all with me. Let's have a big stomp your feet if you agree with the leaders that this is the way God is leading the church because that is easy. We could have a big hoopla and get all excited and blow up balloons and so. I don't want to do that, because I think what we are heading into is, I don't want to treat it in any way in a superficial, I don't want to trivialize it.

So I want to ask you to vote for this vision, but I don't want to ask you to vote now or with a vote with your voice or with your hand. I want to ask you to vote in the following ways over the next five years. First, I want to ask you to vote with your mind. I want you to go home tonight and I want you to think. I mean really think. Who is going to turn this mess of a world around? Who has any answers to be unraveling in the disintegration that we see happening all around the world? The hope of the world, and I have said it a thousand times, the hope of the world is Jesus Christ and His gospel proclaimed through a local church. It is the hope of the world. And I want to ask you to be thoughtful about that. I want to ask you to say, You know what, I can be a part of the redemptive solution of God to a world that is facing problems that it cannot solve. So I want to ask you to think it through with your mind. And vote with your mind to be a part of this church's great adventure in the next five years and just be real calculated about it. And say, I want a significant part of my mind to be engaged in the adventure of world redemption through this five-year plan.

And then I want to ask you to vote with your heart. I want to ask you to get your heart connected to some loving hearts of other people around here in community so that all of what flows out in the next five years will flow out of community. It is easy to get our minds fixed on a cause and to lose a sense of doing it together. I hope and pray that will not happen. I mean, we are going to become a lot more focused and a lot more intentional but not at the loss of community. So I want to ask you to vote with your heart and to put your arms around some folks and say, with our hearts knit together, let's walk in the direction of this great adventure.

And then I am going to ask you to vote with your feet. I talked about engaging in the discipline of assembling. I am going to vote every Wednesday or Thursday night, and I am going to vote every weekend. I am going to vote by showing up, by just getting in the car and by coming and praying and supporting. Vote with your feet.

And then I am going to ask you to vote with your hands. Again, hands that are reached out to lost people. Friends, you have got to have your hand out, in the workplace, in the neighborhood, at the health club. You have got to put your hand out to lost people. And I am going to ask you to roll your sleeves up and work with your hands. To find your spiritual gift and to use it. Vote with your hands.

And vote with your lips. I am going to ask you to pray and to pray every day that we will achieve this plan for God's glory. Pray every day that we will push back the forces of evil and that with God's help we will achieve these objectives. And I want to ask you with your lips to worship. To come and just push back the forces of evil with the sheer volume of worship and praise that just turns the evil one to running. Just vote with your lips.

And then I want you to vote with your daytimers. I want you to rearrange your priorities and your schedules so that you seek first the kingdom of God. If you wind up five years from now and you say, You know what? I squandered the run; I just squandered it. I went out and I did that which was okay and I did a little of that and a little of that. I just didn't do the best part. I just never rearranged my life so that I was elbow deep in the best part. Vote with your daytimer.

And finally, vote with your checkbook. Resolve not to miss a single full tithe in this entire five-year run. I hope all of you are taking the teaching on the weekend seriously these days. You rearrange your finances and you say one thing I will not do is rob God or rob this church of the resources it will take to achieve these plans. Rearrange your finances so that you can at least get the full tithe to the work of God here so that we can unleash resources to achieve these objectives. And those of us who have a measure of affluence, now with clear objectives, if we have some extra earning power, let's earn a little extra and let's throw it into the pot and let's say that these are worthy objectives and that it is worth putting some extra resources into. But I will tell you this, friends, if you vote that way, with your mind and your heart and your feet and your hands and your lips and your schedules and your checkbook, with that kind of investment someday we will achieve these objectives and Christ will be honored and you will be glad. And in heaven when we are all together forever all of us will say, You know that five-year run, that run from the twentieth anniversary to the twenty-fifth anniversary, what a ride, what an adventure, and we did it together.

Let's stand for closing prayer. And now as just a sign of unity, would you take the hand of someone next to you, and let's just connect all throughout the auditorium. Reach across the aisles, and let's commit what we believe are God's plans for the next five years. Just commit them to God. Oh God, I am so grateful that you lead, that you guide, that when leaders humble themselves and bow and pray and discuss, that you lift us out of our petty preoccupations, you lift us out of our comfort levels. You show us a world. You show us your power. You remind us of what our lives are to be about and you give us a dream and you give us a vision and you call us to pursue it with all of our hearts. So Lord, here we are, hand in hand, heads bowed. May the gun go off. May you be honored and glorified and receive all of the praise when these goals are achieved. And may we just enjoy the adventure and talk about it for eternity. And everybody agreed together and said, Amen. Thanks everybody.

Recorded by the Prestonwood Pulpit,
Prestonwood Baptist Church,
15720 Hillcrest, Dallas, TX 75248

Notes

Introduction

1. For more discussion of this critical concept, see Aubrey Malphurs, *Values-Driven Leadership* (Grand Rapids: Baker, 1996).

2. See Aubrey Malphurs, *Developing a Dynamic Mission for Your Ministry* (Grand Rapids: Kregel, 1998).

3. See Aubrey Malphurs, *Strategy 2000* (Grand Rapids: Kregel, 1996).

Chapter 1 It's a Must!

1. George Barna, "The Man Who Brought Marketing to Church," *Leadership* (Summer 1995): 125.

2. See Aubrey Malphurs, *Planting Growing Churches for the 21st Century* (Grand Rapids: Baker, 1992), chap. 8.

Chapter 2 What Are We Talking About?

1. For a more in-depth treatment of these differences, see Malphurs, *Developing a Dynamic Mission for Your Ministry*, 48–57, and Aubrey Malphurs, *Ministry Nuts and Bolts* (Grand Rapids: Kregel, 1997), chap. 7.

2. John R. W. Stott, "What Makes Leadership Christian?" *Christianity Today*, August 1985, 24.

3. Marcus Buckingham, *One Thing You Need to Know* (New York: Free Press, 2005), 59.

Chapter 3 The Vision Personnel

1. An exception is the person who is starting a new ministry, such as a church planter in a "cold start" (no initial core group). He will develop the vision and invite others to join him in accomplishing this vision.

2. For an in-depth treatment of this issue, see Aubrey Malphurs, *Doing Church: A Biblical Guide for Leading Ministries through Change* (Grand Rapids: Kregel, 1999).

3. Peter Wagner provides an excellent discussion of this concept and its historical development in America in his book *Leading Your Church to Growth* (Ventura, CA: Regal, 1984), 73–105.

4. Isabel Briggs Myers, *Gifts Differing* (Palo Alto, CA: Consulting Psychologists Press, 1980), 2.

5. Isabel Briggs Myers and Mary H. McCaulley, *Manual: A Guide to the Development and Use of the Myers-Briggs Type Indicator* (Palo Alto, CA: Consulting Psychologists Press, 1985), 45, 47.

6. The MBTI can be administered at most psychological counseling centers and some assessment centers. It should be administered only by someone who has met all the qualifications of the Association for Psychological Type (APT).

7. To obtain a copy of the *Kiersey Temperament Sorter*, contact Prometheus Nemesis Book Company, P.O. Box 2748, Del Mar, CA 92014; 800-754-0039.

8. Myers and McCaulley, *Manual*, 14.

9. Jay Conger, *The Charismatic Leader* (San Francisco: Jossey-Bass, 1989), 65.

10. James M. Kouzes and Barry Z. Posner, *The Leadership Challenge* (San Francisco: Jossey-Bass, 1987), 94.

11. Fred Smith, *Learning to Lead* (Waco, TX: Word, 1986), 38.

12. Ibid.

Chapter 4 The Vision Process

1. In my work with students at Dallas Theological Seminary, I have discovered exceptions among those who score Ss and Cs on the *Personal Profile* but show a preference for intuition on the *Myers-Briggs Type Indicator* (MBTI).

2. If you are not able to locate this tool in your area, call the Carlson Company at 800-777-9897 for assistance or look for information online.

3. John Haggai, *Lead On!* (Waco, TX: Word, 1986), 14.

4. Warren Bennis and Burt Naus, *Leaders* (New York: Harper & Row, 1985), 95.

5. Ibid., 96.

6. Pastor Stevens's material in this chapter is used by permission.

7. Bill Bright, *Come Help Change the World* (San Bernardino, CA: Here's Life Publishers, 1979), 7.

8. John Madden, with Dave Anderson, *Hey, Wait a Minute* (New York: Ballantine, 1985), 225–26.

9. See my rationale for this in *Advanced Strategic Planning* (Grand Rapids: Baker, 1999).

10. In my book *Ministry Nuts and Bolts*, 121–31, I not only present these vision statements but critique them as well.

Chapter 5 It's a Vision!

1. For further discussion of what pastors and churches can and cannot do, see my book *Doing Church.*

2. George Gallup Jr., *The Unchurched American—Ten Years Later* (Princeton, NJ: The Princeton Religion Research Center, 1988), 3.

3. "NetFax at 100 . . . Learnings from the Past," *NetFax*, no. 100 (June 22, 1998): 1.

4. George Barna, *Successful Churches: What They Have in Common* (Glendale, CA: The Barna Research Group), 15.

5. Conger, *The Charismatic Leader*, 78.

6. Kouzes and Posner, *The Leadership Challenge*, 123–24.

7. Ibid., 124.

Chapter 6 Overcoming Initial Inertia

1. John P. Kotter, *A Force for Change* (New York: The Free Press, 1990), 7.

2. Ibid., 5.

3. Ibid., 4.

4. Ibid., 5.

5. Kouzes and Posner, *The Leadership Challenge*, 137–38.

6. Ibid., 153.

7. John Naisbitt and Patricia Aburdene, *Megatrends 2000* (New York: William Morrow, 1990), 227.

8. Ibid.

Chapter 7 Overcoming Obstinate Obstacles

1. Conger, *The Charismatic Leader*, 108.

2. Ibid.

3. Ibid., 109.

4. Robert S. McGee, *The Search for Significance* (Houston: Rapha Publishing, 1990), 15.

5. Ibid., chap. 6.

6. Ibid., chap. 7.

7. Ibid., chap. 8.

8. Ibid., chap. 9.

9. For more information on the divine design concept, see Aubrey Malphurs, *Maximizing Your Effectiveness* (Grand Rapids: Baker, 1996).

10. This is one of the statements my friend Pastor Bruce Bugby, of Willow Creek Community Church, has used to communicate this concept.

11. Robert E. Coleman, *The Master Plan of Evangelism* (Grand Rapids: Revell, 1963), 43.

12. Ibid., 40–41.
13. Kouzes and Posner, *The Leadership Challenge*, 218.
14. Ibid., 221.
15. Ibid., 195.
16. Ibid., 260.
17. Ibid., 242.
18. Ibid., 260, 263.

Chapter 8 Bittersweet

1. Good risks are hard to determine and vary from person to person. What may be a good risk for one leader may not be for another. Tom Peters has a brief but helpful discussion of what I call good risk taking in *Thriving on Chaos* (New York: Harper & Row, 1987), 322–23.

2. Joel Arthur Barker, *Discovering the Future: The Business of Paradigms* (St. Paul, MN: ILI Press, 1985), 30–31.

Index

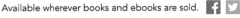

ALSO AVAILABLE FROM
AUBREY MALPHURS . . .

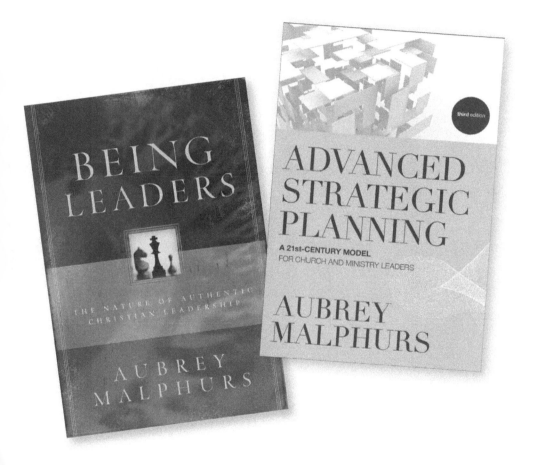